EXTRAORDINARY RECIPES FROM

PORTLAND, MAINE CHEF'S TABLE

MARGARET HATHAWAY

Photography by Karl Schatz

CASCO BAY

LYONS PRESS
Guilford, Connecticut

An imprint of Globe Pequot Press

To buy books in quantity for corporate use
or incentives, call **(800) 962–0973**
or e-mail **premiums@GlobePequot.com.**

Lyons Press is an imprint of Globe Pequot Press.

All photos by Karl Schatz unless otherwise noted

Editor: Amy Lyons
Project Editor: Tracee Williams
Text Design: Libby Kingsbury
Layout Artist: Nancy Freeborn

Library of Congress Cataloging-in-Publication Data is available on file.

ISBN 978-0-7627-8044-0

Printed in the United States of America

10 9 8 7 6 5 4 3 2 1

Restaurants and chefs often come and go, and menus are ever-changing. We recommend you call ahead to obtain current information before visiting any of the establishments in this book.

For Sadie

Chef Bob Smith, 1961–2010

CONTENTS

Acknowledgments

Just as Portland's food scene is a collaborative endeavor, this book has been the work of many. The greatest thanks go to the incredible chefs and restaurateurs who make Portland their home. Your generosity in sharing stories and recipes, and in making time for Karl to photograph your faces, kitchens, and beautifully plated dishes, has been astounding. We feel honored to know you and eat your food, and humbled to attempt its re-creation in our own kitchen.

For wonderful suggestions and unfailing great taste, thanks to Don and Samantha Hoyt Lindgren. For help testing and scaling recipes, special thanks go to Elise Richer, mathematician, baker, and home chef extraordinaire. Thanks also to Allison Duffy, Katherine Endy, and Joe Silberlicht for their careful testing, thoughtful comments, and candid opinions.

Thanks to my supremely patient editor, Amy Lyons, for suggesting the project, and for giving us an excuse to hire a sitter and go out to dinner—all in the name of research. Thanks to Tracee Williams and her team for putting together such a beautiful book, and to Ann Marlowe for her knowledgeable and thorough copy editing. Thanks also to my agent, Jill Grinberg, for her guidance, diligence, and steady support.

Thanks to the Portland Observatory, especially Mark Shapp, and to Lambert Coffin Attorneys at Law for allowing Karl to photograph the city from your highest peaks.

We're grateful to Nick Branchina at Browne Trading Company for sharing knowledge of the working waterfront, and for connecting us to the Portland Fish Exchange. At the Portland Fish Exchange, thanks go to Bert Jongerden for letting Karl photograph the auction in action. On the photo front, thanks also go to Urban Farm Fermentory for the mead, Free Range Fish & Lobster for the lobster, Harbor Fish Market for their iconic facade, Maine Root for the root beer, Bam Bam Bakery for the whoopie pies, and the farmers of the Portland Farmers' Market—the food you grow photographs beautifully and tastes even better.

To Jody Fein, Robb and Luisa Hetzler, and Jack Flagler, thanks for your continued support through another book—from spending time with the kids to testing recipes to sampling the goods at restaurants around town, we couldn't have done this without you!

Thanks to the great staff at Aurora Photos for tolerating many "long lunches." Thanks to Donna Picard for putting up with a crazy carpooling schedule.

To Jen Gilbert and the Back Cove Midwives, thanks for once again guiding us through the dual gestation of book and baby. One of these days, we'll stop doing them in pairs.

Thanks to our children, Charlotte, Beatrice, and Sadie (formerly known as Piggy Wiggle), for their patience as we juggled everyone's schedules and tried to keep our lives organized. We promise a future of less pork belly—and the kitchen whiteboard will be yours soon.

Finally, thanks to the amazing farmers, foragers, and fisherpeople of Maine. Without you, we would have no food to write about. Echoing our friends at Broadturn Farm, we say thank you and "Blessings on the meal."

Introduction

On a Sunday afternoon each fall, a tent is erected in a fallow field at Cape Elizabeth's Turkey Hill Farm. Beneath it, two dozen of Portland's best chefs gather for their annual fundraiser for Cultivating Community, a local nonprofit dedicated to strengthening urban communities by growing and preparing food. Over the years, the changing group of chefs have come together in sparkling sun, pouring rain, and ocean mists, donating their time and knife skills to create a "Twenty Mile Meal" made from ingredients raised on the farm and supplied by producers within twenty miles of Portland. No matter the weather, diners flock to the farm, sampling their way around dishes that range from scallop ceviche and kelp slaw to pork raised just feet away, and washing it all down with cider, pressed on-site from the fruit of heirloom apple trees that dot the farm. Though Turkey Hill is outside the city limits, the meal is emblematic of Portland's dynamic and collaborative food culture: participating chefs chat with each other, bring their children, and take breaks to sample and compliment each other's food, while supportive patrons come out to share the bounty. This, in a nutshell, is the Portland food scene.

Stretched along the shores of picturesque Casco Bay, the city of Portland boasts an astonishing concentration of great restaurants and a food community with a sense of camaraderie and purpose. On the city's main peninsula—which reaches from the Munjoy Hill neighborhood and its Eastern Promenade at one side to the West End, edged by the mouth of the Fore River, at the other—sit nearly one hundred restaurants, spanning a great diversity of flavors, enthusiasms, and price points. Though the city's many tourists often associate the food of Portland with the lobster and chowder spots that jut on wharfs over the working waterfront, just a few blocks inland the city is home to an array of cuisine that, in 2009, resulted in Portland being named the Foodiest Small Town in America by *Bon Appétit* magazine.

The reasons for this culinary convergence are many. Portland's geographical situation—water on both sides and close proximity to the farms of southern Maine—gives chefs access to a great variety of local ingredients, from grass-fed beef to farmstead cheeses to the daily catch coming in on countless fishing boats. The area's farm-to-table movement began decades ago, urged on by the Maine Organic Farmers and Gardeners Association, the first organization of its kind in the country, and a group of which many Portland chefs are proud to be members. This connection between growers and chefs has encouraged the cultivation—and, in some cases, resurrection—of heirloom ingredients; don't be surprised to find salsify, burdock root, husk cherries, and Tolman Sweet apples on menus around town. The access and commitment to using local ingredients, in a region with such harsh winters and short growing seasons, has also led chefs to experiment with methods of food preservation. It's not uncommon to find house-made preserves and pickles, as well as charcuterie cured on-site, at restaurants throughout Portland.

BLUEBERRIES

Tiny, juicy, and intensely flavorful, wild blueberries are one of Maine's most delectable summer treats. Their scrubby plants dot roadsides around the state, marked by soft green foliage and clumps of white, bell-shaped flowers in June that become dark, sweet berries by the August harvest, then turn the color of flame as the fall progresses. North of Bar Harbor, along the Down East coast, more than 60,000 acres of wild blueberries grow in fields and barrens, where they're managed and harvested by farmers who export this delicacy around the country. In the rest of the state, Mainers still go picking in the manner immortalized by Robert McCloskey in his classic children's book *Blueberries for Sal,* fanning out with pails over reliable hills and bringing quarts of berries home to make jams and pies. Look for blueberries in season at markets and roadside stands, and any time of year frozen, dried, and in preserves.

Beyond ingredients, the city of Portland itself has shaped its vibrant cuisine. Rich in history, reaching back beyond the first European settlement in 1633 to the Abenaki Native Americans who originally lived on the peninsula, Portland has been subject to regular periods of reinvention, brought on over the years by four devastating fires and, more recently, by a combination of immigration and urban renewal. The city's motto, *Resurgam,* Latin for "I will rise again," and the phoenix depicted on its seal are references to the series of fires that destroyed the town in its first centuries. The historic Old Port, with its cobbled streets and charming brick buildings, was built after the most recent fire, on Independence Day of 1866. Around that time, construction flourished throughout the peninsula, giving the city Deering Oaks Park, a narrow-gauge railway, and an abundance of stately, architecturally significant homes. Though a hundred years of sprawl and suburban expansion ensued, the last two decades of the twentieth century brought revitalization to downtown Portland: residential neighborhoods like Munjoy Hill and the West End experienced dramatic gentrification, the Arts District on Congress Street saw the construction of a new building complex for the Portland Museum of Art by the firm of I. M. Pei, and the Old Port was transformed into the area of boutiques and restaurants it is today.

The period also saw an influx of immigrants from near and far: a growing African population came to escape oppressive conditions in their homelands, while Americans from urban centers came to Portland drawn by Maine's state motto, "The way life should be." Despite its small size—fewer than 70,000 inhabitants in the city proper—Portland balances a thriving cultural life with a commitment to ecological conservation. The city supports a symphony and a ballet company, a world-class art museum, and, of course, its vivid culinary scene, while also living up to its former nickname, the

Forest City, dotting the town with green spaces that include pockets of woods, the Fore River Sanctuary, and Portland Trails, a system of connected walking trails. With a population of such diverse interests, it's fitting that Portland would have an equally varied food scene.

In organizing this book, we've chosen to focus on Portland's original peninsula, including restaurants from Munjoy Hill and the East End, the Old Port, the Arts District, the Bayside District, and the West End. Though they're just blocks away from each other, each neighborhood has a distinctive feel. Munjoy Hill is marked by the Eastern Promenade, a steeply sloped park with a view of Casco Bay's islands, forts, and marina that ends in a sandy beach. Home to the Portland Observatory, a wooden signal tower and weather station that was built at the crest of the hill in 1807, Munjoy Hill is crowned by meticulously restored clapboard captain's houses, endowed with large windows and widow's walks. The Old Port, along the waterfront at the base of Munjoy Hill, is Portland's historic center and tourist hub, a district of pedestrian walkways and renovated brick warehouses, and the heart of the city's food scene. Here the smells of wood smoke and sautéing garlic mingle with the briny ocean breeze, and through open doors and plate glass windows, chefs can be seen at work in their kitchens. Heading west on Congress Street, past Monument Square and its statue to the city's fallen soldiers and sailors, the Arts District includes the Maine College of Art, the Portland Museum of Art, and galleries and art spaces intermingled with hip eateries and coffee roasteries. Further inland, near the marshy Back Cove, the Bayside District

THE DAILY CATCH

Perched at the edge of Casco Bay, Portland's working waterfront has for centuries been an integral part of the city's life. In the briny morning mist, boats come in along the pilings of each wharf, unloading their haul of the Gulf of Maine's best, from haddock and cod to monkfish, eel, pollack, and the ubiquitous lobster. Since 1986 the nonprofit Portland Fish Exchange has run a daily auction, organized to ensure fair prices and provide impartial grading and weighing of seafood, and fishmongers from Portland and beyond can be found bidding on the daily catch.

For the public, a stroll down Commercial Street and the adjacent wharves will bring the clean whiff of fresh fish and stops at the famed **Browne Trading Company** (Merrill's Wharf; 800-944-7848), known for the custom-cured seafood from its boutique smokehouse and its extensive selection of caviar, and **Harbor Fish Market** (9 Custom House Wharf; 800-370-1790), owned and operated by the Alfiero family since 1969, with a storefront so iconic it's been featured in countless advertisements, paintings, and postcards.

is an industrial area in the midst of renovation, home to a handful of culinary gems tucked between mattress warehouses and city snowplow storage. Finally, at the far West End of the peninsula, Longfellow Square is marked by a statue of the poet, a Portland native, and historic brick townhouses line the curving streets.

While the city of Portland now extends beyond the "great neck" first settled by the Abenaki, it's striking that so many wonderful restaurants can be found within walking distance of each other. (The Old Port's Wharf Street alone boasts more nationally acclaimed restaurants than many entire cities.) Strolling the length of the peninsula along Congress Street, a hungry visitor can stop for a homemade baguette, a burger made from heritage Scottish Highland beef, braised wild boar over coconut rice, house-cured tempura-fried bacon, fish tacos on homemade tortillas, a slice of mashed potato pizza, a bite of vegan chocolate pie, a bowl of squash ravioli in sage butter, curried beef penang, and a fried green tomato BLT. A few blocks in any direction and the choices grow exponentially.

OFF THE PENINSULA

While the greatest concentration of Portland's restaurants can be found on the peninsula that stretches from Munjoy Hill to the West End, the surrounding neighborhoods and small towns offer their own culinary delights. Across the Casco Bay Bridge, bakeries, brunch spots, gourmet takeout, and seasonal ice cream and lobster shacks can be found in South Portland and Cape Elizabeth. To the north and west, ethnic markets—from Scandinavian to South Asian—abound, as do beloved neighborhood fixtures that specialize in everything from baked goods to beer. Slightly farther afield, many of the farms that supply Portland's restaurants are located just a few miles beyond the city limits. No matter where you find yourself in the Portland metro area, chances are good that you'll be near a great meal.

This book is an invitation to explore Portland through its unique flavors, and through Karl's beautiful photographs of the city. When making the recipes, we hope you'll keep a few things in mind: While we've tried to scale all the dishes to serve four to eight people, some, notably the cured meats, simply must be made on a larger scale. If you plan to make something like Chef Rob Evans's Air-Cured Lomo (page 108), or Chef Jason Loring's House-Brined Corned Beef (page 122), note that you'll need to start more than a month before you plan to serve the meat, but that there are very few things more impressive at a party than homemade charcuterie. In a similar vein, infused vodkas (Sonny's, page 163) must be made in large quantity, but the results will keep and, if decanted into smaller bottles, make lovely gifts. At the opposite end of the spectrum, some cocktails in the book are meant to be assembled individually, and make a single serving. As with any recipe, feel free to adjust seasonings and ingredients to taste, though with cured meats it's best not to change proportions of salt, sugar, and liquid in the brine.

If you've visited Portland, perhaps you'll find the recipe for an amazing dish you tasted. If you haven't yet made it to Casco Bay, we hope this book will inspire you to take a trip north.

Artemisia Cafe

61 Pleasant Street
(207) 761-0135
www.artemisiacafe.com
Chef/Owner: Celia Bruns

On the ground floor of a building that's been occupied by a bakery and by the Maine College of Art and currently holds studio space for a group of local artists, Artemisia Cafe blends a light, imaginative breakfast and lunch menu with a bohemian vibe—local art hangs on the walls, salvaged window panes dangle on chains from the ceiling, artists sneak in past the kitchen through a door to the studios. Fittingly, chef/owner Celia Bruns named the cafe for both the feminist Italian Baroque painter Artemisia Gentileschi and the family of herbs bearing the same name (which includes wormwood, the foundation of absinthe).

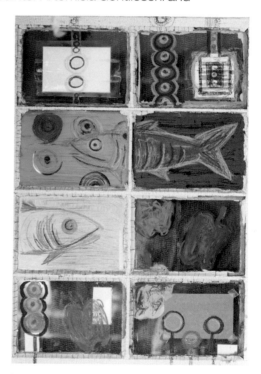

Opened in 2000, the cafe began as a serendipitous confluence of events: over the course of two weeks, Chef Bruns, who was then managing a local restaurant, learned of a cafe in the space that was going out of business, went to look at it on a whim, was offered the space by the building's owners, and then was offered a bank loan that made the dream a reality. As she says now, "Everything happened so quickly that I didn't have time to realize how crazy it was!" Though she'd spent most of her restaurant training in the front of the house, Chef Bruns quickly developed a menu of what she calls "comfort food with a twist," taking inspiration from various countries and influences. Some of the original menu is still offered, notably the grilled sweet potato sandwich, an addictive combination of slices of sweet potato on multigrain bread with avocado, sprouts, red onions, tomato, and lemon poppy seed mayonnaise. Other popular menu items range from a Veggie Dumpling Salad with Asian Slaw and Ginger Soy Dressing to the Turkey and Stuffing Sandwich with Cranberry Mayo, bringing Thanksgiving to Portland year round. On weekends Artemisia is open for brunch, and Chef Bruns's egg dishes, from Oeufs en Meurette to Huevos Rancheros, are well worth the inevitable wait.

Both the Sunny Tartine and the Grilled Shrimp and Artichoke Sandwich below include a sauce or spread that can be made in advance and is versatile enough to serve with other meals. Try the Lutenica sauce, a traditional puree of roasted vegetables, sometimes called ajvar, that's popular in Bulgaria and the Balkans, with grilled chicken or fish or as a dip for vegetables. Chef Bruns's take on artichoke spread is wonderful as a dip, with seafood, or simply spread on toast.

Sunny Tartine

AN OPEN-FACED SANDWICH

(MAKES 6 SANDWICHES)

For the Lutenica sauce (makes approximately 3 cups):

20 ounces jarred roasted red peppers

1 small eggplant, peeled and cubed

½ cup diced carrots

1 (10-ounce) can tomato puree

1 tablespoon balsamic vinegar

1 red chili, minced

¼ cup brown sugar

½ cup extra virgin olive oil

Salt and freshly ground black pepper

For the sandwiches:

2 medium zucchini, sliced diagonally into rounds
  ¼ inch thick

4 portobello mushroom caps, sliced ½ inch thick

1 medium red onion, halved and thinly sliced

Extra virgin olive oil

Salt and freshly ground black pepper

5 tablespoons unsalted butter, softened

6 slices hearty bread

12 eggs

1 cup Lutenica sauce

1 cup baby spinach

½ cup goat cheese

Chopped herbs for garnish (a combination of basil,
  chives, and parsley)

To make the Lutenica sauce: Drain the roasted red peppers and rinse well. Chop the peppers and set aside.

Preheat oven to 400°F. Scatter eggplant cubes in a single layer in a baking dish and cover tightly with foil. Roast eggplant in oven until soft, approximately 20 minutes.

While eggplant is roasting, place carrots in a small pot with enough water to cover and boil until soft, then drain.

Combine chopped red peppers, roasted eggplant, and boiled carrots in the bowl of a food processor. Add tomato puree, balsamic vinegar, red chili, and brown sugar and pulse until a few chunks remain. While the processor is running, pour olive oil in a thin stream, blending until incorporated but still a little chunky. Season with salt and pepper to taste.

To make the sandwich: Brush zucchini, mushroom, and onion slices with olive oil and sprinkle with salt and pepper. Grill until just soft, turning once.

Thinly spread the softened butter on each side of the bread slices, using ½ tablespoon per slice,and grill lightly, turning once. While bread is grilling, melt remaining 2 tablespoons of butter on a well-seasoned skillet or griddle (or in a large nonstick skillet) and cook eggs sunny side up until the yolks are barely set. If using a skillet, work in batches, making sure not to crowd the pan.

To assemble the sandwiches: Spread Lutenica sauce on each slice of bread, top with baby spinach and grilled vegetables, and carefully slide two eggs onto the top of each sandwich. Drizzle with a little more Lutenica sauce and sprinkle crumbled goat cheese and herbs over the top.

GRILLED SHRIMP & ARTICHOKE SANDWICH

(MAKES 6 SANDWICHES)

For the artichoke spread (makes approximately 2 cups):

1 cup mayonnaise

½ cup crumbled feta cheese

½ cup chopped artichoke hearts from a can, drained and well rinsed

2 cloves garlic, minced

1 tablespoon freshly ground black pepper

For the sandwiches:

6 sandwich-size baguettes or ciabatta rolls

5 tablespoons extra virgin olive oil

30 jumbo shrimp

1 teaspoon smoked hot paprika

4 cups fresh spinach leaves (approximately 6 ounces)

Salt and freshly ground black pepper

1 cup artichoke spread

10 ounces jarred roasted red peppers, drained, rinsed well, and sliced

12 slices aged provolone cheese

To make the artichoke spread: Mix all ingredients in a bowl. Cover with plastic wrap, and let set in the refrigerator for at least 1 hour. Artichoke spread can be made ahead and will keep for a week in the refrigerator.

To make the sandwiches: Slice baguettes or ciabatta rolls in half, brush with 1 tablespoon of the olive oil, and lightly grill, cut side down. Shell and clean the shrimp, removing tails and patting dry. In a bowl, toss the shrimp with 2 tablespoons olive oil and the smoked paprika. Skewer the shrimp and grill until just cooked through, approximately 5 minutes, turning once.

De-stem the spinach, rinse well, and pat dry. Working in batches in a large skillet over medium-high heat, sauté spinach in remaining 2 tablespoons olive oil and season to taste with salt and pepper.

To assemble the sandwiches: Spread a thick layer of artichoke spread onto the bottom half of each roll. Top with sautéed spinach, sliced roasted red peppers, 5 grilled shrimp, and 2 slices provolone cheese. Place sandwich halves under the broiler just long enough to melt the cheese, then top with the other half of the roll.

Aurora Provisions

64 Pine Street
(207) 871-9060
and
Museum Cafe by Aurora Provisions
Portland Museum of Art
(207) 775-6148 ext. 3203
www.auroraprovisions.com
Chef/Owner: Marika Kuzma

Creating "beautiful food for busy people," the West End's Aurora Provisions started out in the 1990s as Portland's answer to Dean and Deluca, selling inventive salads and entrees by the pound, cookies and desserts by the piece, gourmet groceries, and a well-chosen selection of wines. Since Chef Marika Kuzma bought the business in 2001, Aurora Provisions has expanded its offerings to include a bustling lunch service—Wednesday's Macaroni and Three Cheeses crowds the house—and a thriving catering business. In 2011 they also began operating the cafe at the Portland Museum of Art, serving light meals in the museum's lower level in a space surrounded by antique china and cut glass.

The menu at the restaurant changes daily, depending upon what's been delivered by the local farms that provide most of their produce, but a few things are constant: Bob's Legendary Raspberry Scones have such a following that they're usually gone by 9 A.M., and the Parisian Street Sandwich—thinly sliced ham, brie, microgreens, and cornichons on baguette—is a perennial lunch favorite. Chef Kuzma's aesthetics match her culinary leanings, and a sense of beauty and abundance prevails, from the refrigerated case,

where take-out salads are mounded on platters adorned with greens and flowers, to the grocery displays, where baskets of local produce are tucked beneath the counter and European and Maine-made artisan chocolates are presented on tiered porcelain platters.

The soup of the day often reflects what's seasonally available, and the borscht is a fall favorite. Drawing on Chef Kuzma's Ukrainian roots, it's adapted from her mother's recipe, and its earthy flavors are perked up by a generous addition of fresh herbs. The Chocolate Zucchini Cake is a wonderful way to use the last zucchini in the garden, which give it a moist texture. When buying chocolate, Chef Kuzma recommends choosing the best possible—don't skimp on cocoa content and keep in mind that the better the chocolate, the better the cake.

Mama Kuzma's Beet & Wild Mushroom Borscht
(SERVES 8)

1¾ pounds purple beets

1 cup dried wild mushrooms

4 tablespoons (½ stick) unsalted butter or extra virgin olive oil

1 medium onion, finely diced

2¼ teaspoons finely minced garlic

12 ounces tomato juice

3 quarts vegetable stock

1½ bay leaves

½ cup plus 2 tablespoons sugar

1½ tablespoons kosher salt

1½ teaspoons freshly ground black pepper

¼ cup red wine vinegar

1 cup finely chopped fresh dill

1 cup finely chopped fresh parsley

Chopped dill and parsley for garnish (optional)

Thoroughly scrub beets, trimming tops and tails but leaving skin on. In a large pot over medium-high heat, cook beets in enough boiling water to cover. When beets are fork tender, remove from water and cool completely, then peel and shred on a box grater (or with the grating attachment to a food processor). Set aside.

In a medium-size saucepan, combine dried mushrooms with 1 quart of water and bring to a boil, cooking until mushrooms are soft and tender. Drain, reserving liquid for the soup, and finely dice the mushrooms.

In a soup pot, heat butter or oil over medium heat and sauté onion and garlic until fragrant, about 3 minutes. Add tomato juice, shredded beets, diced mushrooms, and vegetable stock. Cook over medium heat for a few more minutes, then add remaining ingredients, including reserved mushroom liquid. Bring soup to a simmer and cook for 30 minutes. Taste for seasoning and adjust salt if necessary. The finished soup should be well rounded, with a full, earthy flavor. Garnish with fresh herbs before serving, if desired.

Chocolate Zucchini Cake
with Chocolate Cream Cheese Icing

(MAKES ONE 9-INCH ROUND CAKE)

For the cake:

4 tablespoons (½ stick) unsalted butter, softened
½ cup canola oil
2 cups sugar
4 large eggs, at room temperature
1 tablespoon pure vanilla extract
¼ cup orange juice
4 ounces unsweetened chocolate, melted and cooled
1 cup sour cream
2½ cups all-purpose flour
1 tablespoon baking powder
2 teaspoons baking soda
1 teaspoon salt
2 cups grated zucchini
1 cup mini semisweet chocolate chips

For the icing:

8 ounces cream cheese, softened
4 tablespoons (½ stick) unsalted butter, softened
1 cup sifted confectioners' sugar
6 ounces semisweet chocolate, melted and cooled

To make the cake: Preheat the oven to 350°F. Grease and lightly flour two 9-inch round cake pans, and line the bottoms with parchment or waxed paper.

In a large bowl on the medium speed of the mixer, beat together butter, oil, and sugar until light and fluffy, about 3 minutes. Add the eggs one at a time, beating until incorporated. Beat in vanilla, orange juice, melted chocolate, and sour cream.

In a separate bowl, sift together flour, baking powder, baking soda, and salt. Add to batter, beating until just combined. Stir in grated zucchini and chocolate chips.

Pour batter into prepared pans and bake 30–35 minutes, until a toothpick inserted in the center comes out clean. Cool cakes in the pans on a wire rack until room temperature.

To make the icing: Beat butter and cream cheese on the medium speed of a mixer until smooth. Beat in sugar, then gradually add melted chocolate and beat until well incorporated.

To assemble the cake: Remove cooled cakes from pans. Spread icing between layers, then frost sides and top.

BACK BAY GRILL

65 PORTLAND STREET
(207) 772-8833
WWW.BACKBAYGRILL.COM
CHEF/OWNER: LARRY MATTHEWS JR.

In an intimate space that was once a pharmacy and soda fountain and now seats just thirty-four in the main dining room, Back Bay Grill has been a Portland fixture since 1988. Owned for many years by the late Joel Freund, a former attorney and wine connoisseur who worked closely with current chef/owner Larry Matthews Jr. before selling the restaurant to him in 2002, "the Grill" has received national recognition for both its seasonally changing menu and its exquisite wine list. A recipient of the *Wine Spectator*

Award every year since 1998, Back Bay Grill has also earned acclaim from the James Beard Foundation, which invited Chef Matthews to participate in its Discovery Series in 2001 at the tender age of twenty-eight.

The restaurant's menu is inspired by French and Italian cuisine, but as Chef Matthews notes, what he serves is "mostly just simple food cooked entirely from scratch with as many locally sourced products as possible." Though the offerings change regularly, a few dishes never leave the menu, like the grilled flatiron steak with mushroom bordelaise, and the signature crème brulée: silky vanilla cream topped by a crisp amber layer of perfectly caramelized sugar.

Chef Matthews's recipes often include many components, each one essential to the finished dish. Don't be put off by the number of moving parts—simply plan accordingly, take a deep breath, and prepare to savor the results. When making the Crispy Pork Belly, make sure to begin at least two days before you plan to serve the meal, as the pork needs to sit overnight after being seasoned, and again after being roasted. You will have more cured pork belly than needed; slice, sear, and serve leftovers in sandwiches or on a bed of greens. For the Truffled Beef Tartare, use the highest quality of fresh beef tenderloin, preferably pasture raised. When making the accompanying Crispy Egg Yolk, be sure to use an accurate thermometer and a light hand—when perfectly done, the yolk will be crisp on the outside and just barely set inside.

PORTLAND MUSEUM OF ART

In the center of the city's Downtown Arts District, the Portland Museum of Art (7 Congress Square; 207-775-6148), founded in 1882, is Maine's oldest and largest public art institution. Comprised of three linked buildings, the museum is as renowned for its architecture as for its collection: the postmodern façade and main building were designed by Henry Cobb, a partner of I. M. Pei, and built in 1983; the Beaux-Arts L. D. M. Sweat Memorial Galleries were built in 1911, and the Federal-era McLellan House was constructed in 1801. The museum presents works by European masters including Degas, Renoir, and Picasso, as well as a comprehensive collection of Winslow Homer's works and approximately fifteen changing exhibits each year. The PMA is worth a stop on any trip to Portland, and no visit is complete without a treat from the Museum Cafe, operated by Aurora Provisions and serving light luncheon and baked goods.

CRISPY PORK BELLY WITH BUTTERY CARROT PUREE, CURRIED ONIONS & TEMPURA-FRIED CELERY LEAVES

(SERVES 6–8)

For the pork belly:

3 pounds fresh pork belly
Kosher salt and freshly ground pepper, to taste
1 head garlic, roughly chopped
Zest of 1 lemon
5 sprigs fresh thyme

2 carrots, peeled and coarsely chopped
3 ribs celery, coarsely chopped
1 Spanish onion, coarsely chopped
3 cups chicken or duck stock

For the buttery carrot puree:

2 pounds carrots (local, if possible)
½ pound (2 sticks) unsalted butter
2 tablespoons sugar
Water, as needed

For the curried onions:

1 large Spanish onion
2 tablespoons unsalted butter
1 tablespoon curry powder

For the tempura-fried celery leaves:

1 egg
1 cup all-purpose flour
1 cup ice water
Yellow inner leaves of celery heart
Canola oil, for frying

To make the pork belly: Liberally season the pork belly on both sides with the salt and pepper. On the meat side, lay the lemon zest, the garlic, and about half of the thyme. Place in a shallow dish, refrigerate, and allow to sit overnight.

Preheat oven to 350°F. In a large sauté pan, lightly sauté the vegetables and scatter in the bottom of a deep baking dish. Brush any excess salt off the belly, and add the pork to the dish skin side up, along with the zest, garlic, and thyme. Pour the stock into the pan and cover with aluminum foil. Bake for 3½ to 4 hours, until the meat is fork tender. Remove from oven and allow to cool in the braising liquid.

When meat has come to room temperature, place on a flat baking sheet lined with parchment paper, cover with another sheet of parchment paper, and place another flat pan on top. Apply a moderate weight (you can use a couple of unopened cans placed evenly on top), and chill overnight.

To make the buttery carrot puree: Peel and roughly chop the carrots. Place the carrots in a large saucepan, adding butter, sugar, and enough water just to cover. Cook slowly over medium-low heat until the carrots are completely soft. Remove the carrots and thoroughly puree. Set aside.

To make the curried onions: Peel and julienne the onion. In a deep skillet over low heat, melt the butter and add the onion, sweating until thoroughly cooked and soft but not colored. Add the curry powder and continue cooking on low for another 10–15 minutes. Taste and adjust seasonings with salt, freshly ground black pepper, and additional butter.

Make the tempura-fried celery leaves just before serving. In a bowl whisk the egg, flour, and water into a batter. In a pot or deep skillet, heat 2 inches of oil to 325°F. Separate the celery leaves into small clusters and dip them in the batter one cluster at a time and fry in the oil. When crispy, remove from the pot, place on paper towels to blot excess oil, and season with salt to taste.

To serve: Cut the pork belly into portions of 2–3 ounces. In a nonstick pan on very low heat, place each belly portion skin side down and cook until the skin browns nicely and becomes crispy. Flip over with a spatula and finish searing on the other side until warmed through. On each plate, arrange buttery carrot puree, curried onions, and seared pork belly, topping with fried celery leaves.

TRUFFLED BEEF TARTARE
WITH WHITE ANCHOVIES, CRISPY EGG YOLK
& BLACK PEPPER CRACKERS

(SERVES 4)

For the beef tartare:

8 ounces filet mignon
1 teaspoon chopped shallots
1 teaspoon chopped fresh herbs (a combination
    of parsley, tarragon, and chives)
1 tablespoon white truffle oil
1 tablespoon extra virgin olive oil
1 teaspoon sea salt (preferably from Maine)

For the crackers:

1½ cups semolina
1½ cups all-purpose flour
1 teaspoon sea salt (preferably from Maine)
1 cup warm water
⅓ cup extra virgin olive oil
Sea salt, freshly ground black pepper, caraway seeds,
    fennel seeds, for topping (optional)

For the crispy egg yolk:

4 whole eggs, at room temperature
All-purpose flour, for dredging
1 egg beaten with 2 tablespoons water
Finely ground bread crumbs
Canola oil, for frying

For serving:

White anchovies (also called *alici* or *boquerones*)
White truffle oil
Finely chopped fresh herbs

To make the tartare: Finely dice the meat, discarding any chunks of fat. Lay the meat out on waxed paper and place in the refrigerator, uncovered, for about an hour. This will turn the meat a deep red. While meat is chilling, make the crackers and the crispy egg yolks.

To make the crackers: Whisk together the semolina, flour, and salt in the bowl of an electric mixer. Add water and oil and, using the dough hook attachment, mix on low speed until well incorporated, 5–7 minutes. Form into a ball and cut into 12 pieces. (Each piece will make about half a sheet pan of crackers; freeze any remaining dough for later use.) Cover with a damp towel and let dough rest for 30 minutes.

Preheat oven to 375°F. Roll dough to desired thinness (Chef Matthews prefers very thin), poke holes on the top with a fork, and sprinkle with any desired toppings (to serve with beef tartare, Chef Matthews brushes with olive oil and sprinkles with sea salt and black pepper). Place on a parchment-lined cookie sheet and bake for about 10 minutes, until lightly browned.

To make the crispy egg yolks: Place in a medium-size pot enough water to cover the eggs and heat it to 153°F. Add the whole eggs, in the shell, and cook for 1 hour, maintaining temperature. Remove eggs from pot and chill in ice water. When cold, crack the eggs and remove the yolks, making sure to keep them intact, and discard the whites and the shells.

Dredge each yolk in flour, then in the egg wash, and finally roll gently in the bread crumbs. Reserve.

Just before serving, in a pot or deep skillet, bring 2 inches of oil to 360°F.

To serve: Mix the chilled meat in a large bowl with the shallots, herbs, oils, and salt, adjusting seasonings to taste. Divide the meat mixture

between four plates, either forming it into cylinders or simply arranging it on the plate. Fry each egg yolk for about 30–40 seconds, until bread crumbs are crisp and golden, draining briefly on a paper towel before placing on top of the tartare. Arrange a few white anchovies on each plate, and place a few crackers around. Immediately before serving, sprinkle with white truffle oil and some fresh herbs.

FORAGING—FIDDLEHEADS, MUSHROOMS, & RAMPS

For those who know where to look, Maine's forests, fields, and stream banks can provide a bountiful feast. Some of Maine's earthiest and most iconic flavors—from spring's first fiddlehead ferns and wild ramps to autumn's delicate black trumpet mushrooms—are foraged from spots carefully guarded through generations. A fixture on the Portland culinary scene, forager Rick Tibbetts scours southern Maine for these incredible edibles, bringing his haul of unusual fungi and ferns to the area's best restaurants. Delicious on the menu, these natural wonders can also be found at better markets around town. Tempting though it may be to try foraging on your own, it's a skill that requires years of training, and a single false identification can be toxic. Aspiring foragers do best to go on a guided walk with an expert, or to join a foraging club like the Maine Mycological Association (www.mushroomthejournal.com/mma/).

Bar Lola

100 Congress Street
(207) 775-5652
WWW.BARLOLA.NET
CHEF/OWNER: GUY HERNANDEZ
CO-OWNER: STELLA HERNANDEZ

When Princeton-trained architect-turned-chef Guy
Hernandez and his wife Stella, also an architect, opened
Bar Lola in 2006, the couple brought an intentional
ambiguity to the restaurant, starting with the name.
They deliberately chose something with a variety of
associations. As Chef Hernandez notes, "Lola could be
the devil's assistant from *Damn Yankees,* the transvestite
from a Kinks' song, or—as in our family and the Philippines,
where my father is from—it's what you call your
grandmother."

For the food, the couple continue to defy
categorization. They decided to serve small plates, though
they don't consider themselves a tapas bar. They cook
foods inspired by the flavors of Spain, Italy, and France, but
they're not a Mediterranean restaurant. They juxtapose
flavors, building dishes out from their essentials with
unexpected touches, but they're not a fusion restaurant. At base, Chef Hernandez says,
"The honest answer is that we serve the food we like to eat."

Depending on the week, this could include Coffee-and-Cocoa-Rubbed Bistro
Steak with Creamy Rutabaga, or Roasted Heritage Pork Belly with Cabbage and Lime
Slaw, or a riff on a comfort food made by Chef Hernandez's father, affectionately called
Tony's Chicken and Rice, with chicken poached in a fragrant broth of soy, cider vinegar,
bay leaves, peppercorns, and garlic, then browned in a pan and served with rice and a
reduction of the poaching liquid. One constant is the connection to local farmers, who
supply them with everything from root vegetables and greens to half a pig for their son's
fifth birthday. Another constant is the brilliant food—carefully composed, with every detail
in place—which has brought national attention, including being named one of *Travel &
Leisure*'s favorite small places to eat. Though Chef Hernandez can "count on two hands"
the number of nights he's been away from the restaurant since they opened, it's worth it.
As he once wrote in *Maine* magazine, "[to compose] two seven-course meals for a pair
of diners and have them respond to the arc of the meal is extremely rewarding."

For the Poached Oysters in Garlic and Sage Broth, Chef Hernandez recommends
a dense, briny oyster. His preference is for Glidden Points, from the mouth of the
Damariscotta River in midcoast Maine. If you can't find true baby carrots for the Potato
and Baby Fennel Salad with Poached Salmon, Chef Hernandez says don't use the
bagged ones that come out of a tumbler. Simply peel two regular carrots and cut them in
half lengthwise, then into ¾-inch slices on the bias.

POACHED OYSTERS IN GARLIC & SAGE BROTH

(SERVES 6)

1 cup olive oil
8 heads garlic, washed but unpeeled, and
    cut in half horizontally
1 large bunch sage, roughly chopped (about 1 cup)
2 quarts water
2 bay leaves
1 teaspoon red chili flakes
Salt and pepper to taste

2 carrots, finely diced
1 bunch kale, rinsed and sliced into ribbons
4 ribs celery, finely diced

2 dozen oysters (preferably Glidden Points)

In a heavy-bottomed 4-quart pot over medium-high heat, warm the olive oil. Add the garlic and cook until lightly golden. Add sage leaves, water, bay leaves, and chili flakes. Bring to a boil, then reduce heat to simmer, and cook for 20 minutes. Season to taste with salt and pepper. Remove from heat and strain through a fine mesh sieve, discarding solids.

To the strained broth, add carrots, kale, and celery and simmer 10 minutes, or until kale is tender but not mushy. Check seasonings and adjust to taste.

To serve: Shuck 4 oysters into each warm serving bowl. Ladle finished soup over oysters and serve immediately with crusty bread.

CHICKEN TORCHON WITH RED ONION MARMALADE

(SERVES 6)

For the chicken:

4 cloves garlic, minced

¼ cup finely chopped herbs (a combination
of tarragon, parsley, and chives)

4 chicken legs, bones removed

Salt and pepper

For the marmalade:

1 cup red wine vinegar

½ cup sugar

1 teaspoon red chili flakes

1 red onion, peeled, cut in half through the root end,
and thinly sliced

1 baguette, thinly sliced and toasted

Mixed baby greens, for serving

To prepare the chicken: In a small bowl mix garlic
and herbs together. Season each chicken leg
with salt and pepper. Lay chicken legs skin side
down and spread with garlic and herb mixture,
dividing evenly between the four legs. Roll each
leg around the filling and wrap each one tightly
with plastic wrap. Wrap each bundle again with
aluminum foil, twisting the ends to seal.

Bring a medium-size pot of water to a simmer,
and poach the wrapped chicken legs in the water
for 25 minutes. Drain and chill, keeping the legs
wrapped in aluminum foil.

To make the marmalade: Place the vinegar,
sugar, and chili flakes in a small pot and bring to a
boil. Add sliced onions and continue to cook over
medium-high heat for 10 minutes. Remove from
heat, transfer to a bowl, and chill.

To assemble: Unwrap chicken and wipe away
any excess moisture. Slice into ½-inch disks and
serve on crostini topped with greens and a forkful
of the onion marmalade.

Potato & Baby Fennel Salad with Poached Salmon

(SERVES 4)

For the vegetables:

2 pounds baby potatoes, scrubbed (purple potatoes
    from Southpaw Farm are best)
2 tablespoons salt
2 bay leaves
2 bulbs baby fennel, cut in half, fronds removed
    and saved for salmon
2 bunches baby carrots

For the salmon:

½ pound salmon fillet, skin on, pin bones removed
1 cup white wine
1 cup water
Reserved fennel fronds
1 yellow onion, sliced
1 lemon, sliced
Salt and pepper

For the salad:

1 pound mixed baby greens
Olive oil
White wine vinegar
Salt and pepper to taste

To cook the vegetables: Place scrubbed potatoes in a deep, heavy-bottomed saucepan and cover with cold water. Add salt and bay leaves and bring to a boil. Reduce heat, and simmer gently for 10 minutes. Add fennel, and after 5 minutes add carrots. After another 5 minutes, begin checking the potatoes for doneness. When ready, they should be easily pierced with a paring knife but should still have some bite to them. When potatoes are done, drain the vegetables in a colander and rinse with cool water. Cut potatoes and fennel into bite-sized pieces. Set vegetables aside.

To cook the fish: Season salmon with salt and pepper. In a pot just big enough to hold the salmon fillet, combine wine, water, fennel fronds, onion, and lemon. Add the salmon, skin side down, with additional water if salmon is not completely submerged. Bring to a simmer, then turn off heat, leaving fish, vegetables, and water and wine mixture in the pot. Check for doneness after 8 minutes. Gently remove salmon from the poaching liquid and chill.

To assemble the salad: Toss cooled vegetables with baby greens and dress with olive oil and white wine vinegar to taste. Season with salt and pepper. Divide between four chilled plates and top each salad with some of the poached salmon.

MAINE POTATOES

From All-Blue to Onaway, Katahdin to Kennebec, Adirondack Red to Swedish Peanut Fingerlings, Maine potatoes come in all colors, shapes, and sizes. For many years the leading potato producer in the country, Maine still takes pride in her spuds. Thriving in the cool climate and fertile soil of northern Aroostook County, potatoes have been one of Maine's staple foods for centuries and were a leading export since their introduction in the early 1800s. Between 1928 and 1958, Maine grew more potatoes than any other state in the nation, and though production has now declined, Maine potatoes are still beloved by chefs and renowned for their earthy flavor and diverse varieties. Look for them by name on menus and at markets around town.

Bayside Bowl

58 Alder Street
(207) 791-BOWL (2695)
www.baysidebowl.com
Owners: Charlie Mitchell and Justin Alfond
Pastry Chef: Michelle McEwen

Housed on a short one-way street in the formerly industrial Bayside area, in a building that was previously a warehouse for pool tables and pinball machines, Bayside Bowl may seem an unorthodox supper spot. But a few steps from the sheen of the wooden lanes and the crack of balls against pins, the restaurant offers classic American food, made from scratch with plenty of vegetarian options to please the most finicky of bowlers.

Owners Charlie Mitchell and Justin Alfond opened Bayside Bowl in 2010 to bring bowling back to Portland after what they termed "a multi-decade hiatus." What started as a lark has quickly become an institution, with live music on the weekends and nightly leagues, including the tremendously popular Sunday-night restaurant league, which pits staff from various Portland eateries against each other in friendly competition. As one regular puts it, the complete Bayside experience can compress many nights-out into one: "I came down at five to roll a frame, then went to the bar for a drink, then decided to have dinner in the restaurant, then invited another friend down and we caught the show."

In the restaurant, favorites range from pork cigars to a vegan reuben made with smoked tempeh and Maine-made Morse's sauerkraut. But desserts can steal the show. Pastry chef Michelle McEwen, a fifteen-year veteran of kitchens throughout New England, brings sweets center stage (as well as making all the pizza dough and helping with the regular menus and specials). Her Fried Apple Pies are a fun variation on a classic, and are both easy to make and delicious to eat—a strike, especially with a scoop of vanilla ice cream. If you don't want to fry them, Chef McEwen suggests brushing the assembled pies with beaten egg and baking in a 375°F oven until golden brown, then sprinkling with cinnamon sugar and serving warm.

Fried Apple Pies

(MAKES 13 MINI-PIES)

For the rugelach dough:

2¼ cups all-purpose flour

¼ cup confectioners' sugar

Pinch of salt

8 ounces unsalted butter, chilled and diced

8 ounces cream cheese, chilled and diced

For the apple filling:

½ tablespoon unsalted butter

2 large Granny Smith apples, peeled, cored, and diced

¼ cup brown sugar

1 teaspoon ground cinnamon

½ teaspoon ground ginger

1/8 teaspoon ground cloves

Zest of ½ orange

Canola oil for frying
Cinnamon sugar for serving
Vanilla ice cream (optional)

To make the dough: Whisk together in a large bowl the flour, confectioners' sugar, and salt. Using a pastry blender, cut in the butter until it is pea-sized. Cut in the cream cheese and form dough into a ball. Cover in plastic wrap and chill for at least 1 hour.

In a large skillet over medium heat, melt butter and add apples. Cook for 1 minute, stirring regularly. Add sugar, spices, and orange zest and cook for a few minutes, until the apples become tender. Remove from heat and set aside to cool.

To assemble the pies: Lightly flour a work surface and roll out the chilled dough to ¼-inch thickness. Using a 2½-inch round cookie cutter (or the rim of a drinking glass), cut out circles in the dough, making the rounds as close together as possible to avoid wasting dough. Working with one circle at a time, brush the dough with water, then place about ½ tablespoon of filling in the center. Place another circle of dough on top, flattening the edges with your fingers. Using a fork, crimp the edges. When you've assembled all the mini pies, place them on a cookie sheet lined with waxed paper and freeze until they are firm.

In a large heavy-bottomed pot, heat 3 inches of oil to 350°F. Working in batches, being careful not to crowd the pot, fry pies until golden brown. Drain briefly on paper towels to remove excess oil, then sprinkle with cinnamon sugar and serve warm with vanilla ice cream.

BINTLIFF'S AMERICAN CAFE

98 PORTLAND STREET
(207) 774-0005
WWW.BINTLIFFSCAFE.COM
CHEF: NICOLE E. NEAL; OWNERS: JOSEPH AND DIANE CATOGGIO

A Portland institution since it opened in 1989, Bintliff's American Cafe has made brunch into an art. Opened as a five-table cafe by the original owner and chef Roger Bintliff, the restaurant is housed in an historic building at the edge of Deering Oaks Park that has held, over the years, a plumbing supply company, a bank office, apartments, and a number of restaurants (City Hall records date back only to the early 1900s, but it was most likely built in the mid-late 1800s). After a fire in the early 1990s, the space was redesigned by local architect and artist Tony Taylor to its current configuration of two

stories, upper-level outdoor seating, and a Greek Revival façade. Though it's simply the last name of the original owner, patrons often speculate about what a "bintliff" is; a favorite story about Roger Bintliff has a guest asking him what the word means, and another patron at the table chiming in to offer that it's the stick and bag a hobo carries over his shoulder. Bintliff simply smiled, said something polite, and moved on without correcting him.

Current owners Joseph and Diane Catoggio have kept the same cheerful atmosphere since buying the restaurant in 2003, and Chef Nicole Neal has maintained the reputation of the kitchen. Though its seating has expanded, Bintliff's still serves exclusively a brunch menu, but what a menu it is! From sweet to savory, decadent to spartan, there's a meal for every taste. Homemade corned beef hash has a dedicated following far beyond Portland city limits, and other house favorites include Apple Cinnamon Raisin Stuffed French Toast, Grilled Reuben en Phyllo, and Fresh Picked Lobster Benedict. For those whose palates are more austere, there are spelt bagels, fresh fruit bowls, and oatmeal.

Appearing in everything from wraps to omelets to a scrumptious platter with scrambled eggs and dill crème fraiche, Bintliff's Smoked Salmon is one of the house's signature dishes. Easily made in a home kitchen, the salmon will spoil you for store bought. If you're planning to serve it with a weekend brunch, make sure to start brining the fish in midweek, as it needs to soak in the cure, refrigerated, for 48 hours before smoking.

Bintliff's Smoked Salmon

(SERVES 6–8)

¾ cup whole grain mustard

2 large shallots, peeled and chopped

1 packed cup chopped basil

10 ounces granulated sugar (approximately 1½ cups)

5 ounces kosher salt (approximately 1 cup)

1 side of salmon fillet, scaled, pin bones out

3 cups hickory wood chips

In a bowl, mix mustard, shallots, and basil. In a separate small bowl, combine sugar and salt to make the cure. Spread mustard mixture in a nonreactive pan big enough to hold the salmon in one layer, place fish skin side down in the pan, and cover with the sugar-and-salt cure. Wrap pan tightly with plastic wrap, refrigerate, and let cure for 48 hours.

Soak hickory chips in water for 30 minutes.

Remove salmon from refrigerator and rinse in cold water to remove most of the mustard mixture and cure.

Spread soaked hickory chips evenly in the bottom of a separate stainless steel pan. Place a 10-inch springform mold—bottom removed— in the center of the pan. Set a metal grate big enough to hold the fish on top of the springform ring. Place salmon on the grate, skin side down, and cover the entire pan tightly with foil. Place the pan across two gas burners on the stove and turn the heat on both burners to high. As soon as smoke begins to seep from beneath the foil, turn heat to low and set a timer for 20 minutes. When timer goes off, immediately turn off the burners. Leave pan covered and let fish cool completely before removing from the pan.

HOUSE-CURED CHARCUTERIE

Maine's tradition of curing meats and fish goes back centuries, to the Native American techniques chronicled by Henry David Thoreau in his travel classic *The Maine Woods*: "Two stout forked stakes . . . were driven into the ground at each end, and then two poles ten feet long were stretched across over the fire, and smaller ones laid transversely on these a foot apart. On the last hung large, thin slices of moose-meat smoking and drying . . . over the centre of the fire." Though modern meat preservation is more likely to involve Insta Cure ordered online and a metal smoker, the enthusiasm for house-cured meats has been revived throughout Portland's restaurant kitchens. From pork and beef to freshwater trout, cured meats and fish are emerging from smokers, drying rooms, and walk-in refrigerators along the peninsula. Sample them on menus around town, or try your hand at the recipes included in this book.

BLUE SPOON

89 CONGRESS STREET
(207) 773-1116
CHEF/OWNER: DAVID IOVINO

Perched at the top of Munjoy Hill in a storefront that over the last century has housed a barber shop, a pizzeria, a general store, and much more, Blue Spoon is a cozy neighborhood joint of the first class. Stop in on an autumn afternoon and you'll find regulars snacking at the small bar, reading the paper at one of the sidewalk tables, or simply chatting with chef/owner David Iovino, who loves the East End so much that he lives upstairs from the restaurant. The wide windows at the front of the space provide a perfect spot for people watching, while deeper in the building, which Chef Iovino owns, original architectural details—the bead board on the bar, light fixtures in the bathroom— lend a sense of history.

Chef Iovino attended the French Culinary Institute and worked in high-pressure kitchens in New York before moving to Portland a decade ago. Since then, his pace may have slowed, but the food from his kitchen has remained in top form, with a menu that changes regularly, depending on season and whim. One constant is his classic Blue Spoon Burger, made with pasture-raised beef from the Scottish Highland cattle at A Wee Bit Farm, served on house-baked buns, and rated by the *Boston Globe* as one of the top ten burgers in New England. Another wonderful touch comes from the bar, where East End Punch and Watermelon Gin Fizz flow from glass samovars, and frosty homemade limoncello is served by the glass. Despite the name, and the fact that patrons often bring Chef Iovino blue spoons, there's one thing that's curiously absent from the restaurant: blue spoons.

Blue Spoon Burger on House-Made Bun with Warm Potato Salad

BURGERS
(MAKES 7 BURGERS)

1 small Spanish onion, finely diced
1 tablespoon vegetable oil or bacon fat
1 cup red wine
2½ pounds lean ground steak
1 teaspoon salt
½ teaspoon ground black pepper
1½ teaspoons finely chopped rosemary
1 batch Blue Spoon Burger Buns (recipe on next page)

In a medium size skillet over low heat, cook the onions in the vegetable oil or bacon fat until caramelized, stirring occasionally. When onions are golden or dark brown, add red wine to the skillet and cook until pan is completely dry. Place onions in a large bowl to cool.

When onions are room temperature, add ground steak, salt and pepper, and chopped rosemary. Mix well, but be careful not to overmix or the meat will become rubbery when cooked.

Divide mixture into seven balls (weighing approximately 5⅕ ounces each), then flatten balls into ¾-inch thick patties. Season again with salt and pepper. Grill to desired doneness.

Serve on buns, with desired accompaniments and Warm Potato Salad (recipe next page).

BLUE SPOON BURGER BUNS

(MAKES 7–9 BUNS)

½ cup warm water
½ cup milk, at room temperature
1 egg, at room temperature
2 tablespoons extra virgin olive oil
1 tablespoon instant dry yeast
2 tablespoons sugar
2¼ teaspoons salt
2½ cups all-purpose flour
½ cup whole wheat flour
1 egg, lightly beaten
Coarse salt, poppy seeds, or sesame seeds (optional)

In the bowl of an electric stand mixer, combine wet ingredients. Add dry ingredients and mix with the dough hook attachment until mixture is smooth and elastic. Dough should be tacky to the touch.

Put a few drops of oil in a large bowl and scrape in the dough. Cover with a cloth and let rise for 1½ hours, until doubled in bulk. Punch down and roll dough into a long log. Slice into buns weighing approximately 3.2 ounces. Roll into balls on a work surface, using the palm of your hand and rolling until the sides are smooth and tight.

Cover buns with a cloth and let rise for 1½ hours, until dough does not push back when poked.

Preheat oven to 400°F. Brush buns with lightly beaten egg and sprinkle with salt, poppy, or sesame seeds, if desired. Bake at 400°F for 10 minutes, then lower oven temperature to 350°F and bake for an additional 20 minutes.

WARM POTATO SALAD

(SERVES 6–8)

6 Yukon Gold potatoes
2 tablespoons canola oil
1 tablespoon sharp Dijon mustard
1 tablespoon mayonnaise
1 tablespoon extra virgin olive oil
1½ teaspoons aged red wine vinegar
Salt and pepper to taste
Mixed chopped fresh herbs to taste

Preheat oven to 350°F. Prick potatoes with a fork and bake until tender. Cool to room temperature and cut into ¾-inch cubes.

Increase oven temperature to 450°F. Heat canola oil in a large heavy-bottomed skillet over medium-high heat. Add potatoes and fry until golden brown, 5–7 minutes. Drain on paper towels to remove any excess oil, and place in the oven for 10 minutes.

While potatoes are roasting, in a small bowl whisk together mustard, mayonnaise, olive oil, and red wine vinegar. Season with salt, pepper, and chopped herbs to taste.

Place warm potatoes in a large bowl, toss with dressing, and serve.

ARUGULA & POACHED EGG SALAD

(SERVES 4)

Splash of white vinegar
¼ cup extra virgin olive oil
1 cup finely cubed pancetta
2 teaspoons aged red wine vinegar
4 eggs
6 cups arugula
Grana Padano cheese, shaved
Salt and freshly ground pepper to taste

To a large pot with 2 inches of water, add splash of white vinegar. Bring water to a light simmer.

In a small pan, heat the olive oil with the pancetta, slowly rendering the pancetta until crisp. Add red wine vinegar to the pan and put aside.

Working with one egg at a time, crack the egg into a small bowl. Lightly swirl the simmering water and gently pour the egg into the water, being careful not to break the yolk. Cook for a couple of minutes, until the egg is set, not too loose or too firm. Remove from water with a slotted spoon. Pat dry with a clean kitchen towel.

In a large bowl, toss arugula with pancetta and olive oil and red wine vinegar. Divide arugula between four salad plates. Place 1 egg on top of the greens, top with shaved Grana Padano cheese, and season with salt and freshly ground pepper.

BODA

671 CONGRESS STREET
(207) 347-7557
WWW.BODAMAINE.COM
CHEF/OWNER: DANAI "DAN" SRIPRASERT
CO-OWNER: NATTASK "BOB" WONGSAICHUA

"Come experience an eating culture of Thailand," the menu beckons at Boda, the self-described "very Thai kitchen and bar" next to West End landmark Joe's Smoke Shop. Owned by the same team that created the Green Elephant Vegetarian Bistro (page 98), just a few blocks down Congress Street, with a kitchen that is also helmed by chef-owner Danai "Dan" Sriprasert, Boda brings authentic Thai street food to Portland. Chef Sriprasert grew up in his mother's restaurant in Thailand, and though he came to the United States in 2002 to study graphic design, his heart stayed in the kitchen and his palate missed the tastes of home. Building on the success of Green Elephant, he and partner Nattask "Bob" Wongsaichua opened Boda, giving it a name that's evocative of Asia but actually comes from the merging of the owners' adopted "American" names, Bob and Dan.

With a décor that highlights Chef Sriprasert's roots in design—rustic tables and chairs made from wood salvaged from a building in Thailand, natural light from picture windows overlooking Longfellow Square—the menu moves far beyond pad thai. House specialties encourage a broad taste of Thailand, and include Miang Kum Som-oh, bite-sized pummelo fruit salad on betel leaves with toasted coconut, peanut, lime, ginger, shrimp, and shallots in a palm sugar dressing, and Pork Hocks Braised with Star Anise, served with jasmine rice, hard-boiled egg, tofu, Asian mustard green pickles, and spicy-sour chili lime sauce. The kitchen stays open until 1 a.m. to accommodate fellow food service workers, and a late night visit may find servers and sous-chefs from all over Portland relaxing with a Thai Basil Tom Collins and snacking on fried peanuts and taro sticks and Kanom-krok quail eggs.

While many of the ingredients for the Beef Panaeng Curry seem exotic, the lime leaves, fish sauce, galangal, lemongrass, coriander (cilantro) root, and shrimp paste are available at most Asian markets. If you can't find palm sugar (sometimes called arenga sugar or coconut sugar), brown sugar can be substituted.

BEEF PANAENG CURRY

(SERVES 4)

For the curry paste:

¹/₃ cup dried large red chilies

1 teaspoon coriander seeds

1 teaspoon cumin seeds

1 tablespoon unsalted peanuts

2 teaspoons chopped fresh galangal

2 tablespoons sliced lemongrass

1 tablespoon coriander (cilantro) root,
    trimmed and thoroughly scrubbed

2 tablespoons chopped garlic

2 tablespoons chopped shallots

1 teaspoon shrimp paste

1 teaspoon salt

2 cups unsweetened coconut milk

1 pound beef sirloin, thinly sliced and cut into
    1½-inch squares

1 tablespoon shredded lime leaves

2 tablespoons palm sugar

2 tablespoons fish sauce

Coconut cream (optional)

Shredded lime leaves

Thai basil leaves

Thinly sliced red and green chilies

To make the curry paste: Remove seeds from chilies and soak in warm water until softened. Set a skillet over medium heat and, working in batches, separately toast coriander seeds, cumin seeds, and peanuts. Roast each until fragrant, 3–5 minutes. Grind the toasted seeds together in a food processor, then add peanuts, softened red chilies, galangal, lemongrass, coriander root, garlic, shallots, shrimp paste, and salt. Process into a paste. Set aside.

Heat a large skillet over medium-high heat, then add ½ cup coconut milk and bring to a boil. Stir in the curry paste and mix well. Continue stirring until fragrant.

Add the sliced beef and stir well until the meat is covered with the curry mixture, then pour in the remaining 1½ cups coconut milk. Continue stirring until the meat is cooked through then add the lime leaves, fish sauce, and palm sugar. Continue cooking until meat is soft and tender, approximately 20 minutes. If mixture becomes dry, add a bit more coconut milk.

To serve: Drizzle with coconut cream, if you wish, and garnish with shredded lime leaves, a few leaves of Thai basil, and thinly sliced red and green chilies.

Perfect Pairing

THAI BASIL TOM COLLINS

(MAKES 1 GENEROUS COCKTAIL)

Small handful of fresh Thai basil
Freshly squeezed lemon juice
3 ounces gin
2 ounces Homemade Sour Mix (recipe to the right)
Club soda

In a cocktail shaker, muddle Thai basil in a small squirt of lemon juice. Add gin and sour mix and a scoop of ice and shake vigorously. Strain into a chilled martini glass. Top with club soda.

Homemade Sour Mix

Combine equal parts simple syrup and a combination of lemon, lime, and orange juice, adjusted to your taste.

Note: To make simple syrup, place 1 cup granulated sugar and 1 cup water in a saucepan. Over medium heat, stir until dissolved. Cool, and pour into a very clean bottle. Refrigerated, simple syrup keeps indefinitely.

BRESCA

111 MIDDLE STREET
(207) 772-1004
WWW.RESTAURANTBRESCA.COM
CHEF/OWNER: KRISTA KERN DESJARLAIS

Tucked in a narrow downtown storefront, this charming eighteen-seat restaurant is the passion of chef/owner Krista Kern Desjarlais, whose contemporary American menu is, as she puts it, "intensely personal." Named for the Catalan word for honeycomb—a nod both to Kern Desjarlais's background as a pastry chef and to her favorite album by Frank Black—the restaurant combines Kern Desjarlais's varied interests. "The food moves as I move," she notes, explaining her menu's progression through seasons and styles. One constant, however, is Kern Desjarlais's attention to detail. After a career that has taken her to New York, Paris, and Las Vegas, and brought her professional acclaim as a 2010 semifinalist for the James Beard Best Chef Northeast award, she's created Bresca on a scale that allows her to focus on each plate. With a staff of just three, this has presented some challenges: a lengthy maternity leave was impossible, so Kern Desjarlais's daughter Cortland spent much of her early months in the kitchen and still helps her mom shop for Bresca's produce. But the restaurant's size also allows the chef/owner to stay engaged and creative in the kitchen. Opened in 2007, Bresca recently celebrated its fifth anniversary with renovations and a slight reimagining of the menu: more pastry and, after years of exclusively dinner service, a few days a week with earlier hours.

Combining tart vinaigrette with rich chicken livers, the Seared Quail and Vegetables with Liver Vinaigrette makes an impressive and surprisingly quick dinner—perfect for company. Keep in mind that amounts of olive oil and butter can be adjusted to your taste, but be sure not to skimp. Quail is available in better groceries and online at www.vermontquail.com. Cranberry Rose Beignets are delicious on their own, and make an extraordinary autumn dessert with the Chilled Pear Soup. For a fun dinner party, make the soup, cranberry rose filling, and white pepper crème fraiche in advance and let guests help fry the beignets and assemble their desserts.

SEARED QUAIL & VEGETABLES
WITH LIVER VINAIGRETTE

(SERVES 4)

8 small quail

1 cup chicken livers

12 baby carrots

12 baby turnips

20 French green beans

1 cup green peas or broad beans

Olive oil

4 tablespoons sherry vinegar

2 tablespoons port wine

Chicken stock

4 sprigs flat-leaf parsley, chopped

Small bunch chives, chopped

2 shallots, thinly sliced

¼ pound (1 stick) unsalted butter

Salt and freshly ground black pepper

Aged balsamic vinegar, for serving

Maldon sea salt, for serving

Prepare the quail by emptying the cavity, rinsing, patting dry, and trussing with kitchen string. Set aside. Using a sharp knife, clean chicken livers of any membranes, and chop roughly for the sauce. Set aside.

Trim and clean the carrots, turnips, green beans, and peas or broad beans. Working in batches, blanch the vegetables separately in boiling salted water, cooking just until the color deepens, 30–90 seconds.

In a medium size skillet over medium-high heat, add a splash of olive oil and cook the chicken livers until medium rare. Deglaze the pan with sherry vinegar and port, cook until liquid reduces to a syrup, then moisten the pan with a few tablespoons of chicken stock. Add approximately 2 tablespoons of olive oil, the chopped parsley and chives, and the sliced shallots, stirring to mix well. Season with salt and pepper to taste, then remove from heat. Spoon into four individual ramekins for serving.

Heat a warming oven to 250°F. In a large skillet heat 2 tablespoons of olive oil over medium-high heat until it begins to shimmer. Sear the quail, breast skin side down, and cook until juices run clear. Remove from heat, placing entire skillet in warming oven.

In a separate large skillet over medium heat, melt a knob of butter and glaze the blanched vegetables until they are fork tender, seasoning with salt and pepper to taste.

To serve: Divide vegetables evenly among four plates, and top with two quails. Drizzle aged balsamic vinegar over the quails, sprinkle with crunchy Maldon sea salt, and serve liver vinaigrette on the side.

CHILLED PEAR SOUP WITH CRANBERRY ROSE BEIGNET & WHITE PEPPER CRÈME FRAICHE

(SERVES 8)

For the chilled pear soup:

1 pound ripe pears, peeled and chopped

1 cup granulated sugar

1 (3-inch) stick of cinnamon

½ vanilla bean, scraped

2 cups water

1 cup pear juice

Juice of 1 lemon

Pinch of sea salt

For the cranberry and rose filling:

1 pound fresh cranberries

3 cups granulated sugar

Pinch of sea salt

1 cup water

3 tablespoons rose water

For the white pepper crème fraiche:

½ cup crème fraiche

2 tablespoons granulated sugar

⅛ teaspoon freshly ground white pepper

For the beignets:

1 cup ricotta cheese

½ cup all-purpose flour

5 tablespoons granulated sugar

3 tablespoons honey

1 teaspoon vanilla extract

1 teaspoon baking powder

2 eggs

Canola oil, for frying

Cinnamon sugar, for rolling

Powdered sugar, for serving

Candied organic rose petals, for serving (optional)

To make the soup: Combine all ingredients in a large heavy-bottomed pot and simmer over medium-low heat for 10 minutes. Remove from heat and check for sweetness, adding more sugar or lemon juice to taste. Remove cinnamon stick and vanilla bean, and puree soup until smooth. Chill until ready to serve.

To make the cranberry and rose filling: Place cranberries, sugar, sea salt, and water in a medium size saucepan over medium heat and cook until thickened, stirring occasionally. Taste, and adjust sugar if the mixture isn't sweet enough. Remove from heat and cool to room temperature. Stir in rose water, 1 tablespoon at a time, adjusting to taste (you may not use all 3 tablespoons).

To make the white pepper crème fraiche: Combine all ingredients in a small bowl and whisk to a soft mound. Cover with plastic wrap and refrigerate until you're ready to use.

To prepare the beignets: Combine all ingredients in a large bowl to form a wet batter. In a deep skillet, heat 3 inches of canola oil to 350°F. Working in batches, scoop 1 heaping tablespoon of batter into the oil and fry until golden brown. Drain excess oil on paper towels and roll each beignet in cinnamon sugar.

If cranberry and rose filling has cooled to a firm consistency, warm it a little over low heat. Fit a pastry bag with a large enough tip for the cranberries to pass through, and fill the bag with the warmed mixture. Working quickly, plunge the pastry tip into the center of a beignet and pipe a little of the cranberry and rose filling into each, while beignet and filling are still warm.

To assemble the dessert: Divide chilled soup among eight serving bowls. Using two spoons, make quenelles from the white pepper crème fraiche and place a scoop in each bowl. Arrange a beignet on top of the crème fraiche, sprinkle with powdered sugar, and garnish with candied rose petals, if desired. Serve immediately.

Brian Boru

57 Center Street
(207) 780-1506
www.brianboruportland.com
Chef: Brian Clark
Owners: Daniel Steele and Lawrence Kelly

In a big brick building painted vivid red with a Guinness toucan mural covering one side, this traditional Irish pub has been a Portland mainstay for almost two decades. On chilly winter nights the glowing windows of the pub, just blocks from the working waterfront, promise warmth and cheer. Named for the last king of a united Ireland, Brian Boru is a community gathering spot, hosting Irish music sessions and weekly trivia nights, and pouring perfect pints of creamy Guinness. Since Chef Brian Clark's arrival in 2008, the pub's menu has been completely overhauled, incorporating unexpected nose-to-tail dishes with satisfying classics like fish and chips and Reubens piled with house-corned beef. Lamb tacos and hearty cassoulet are favorite menu specials, and Chef Clark,

in a nod to his vegetarian wife, has also made permanent a few veggie entrees, including the excellent Chick Pea Veggie Burger.

While Chef Clark's Sunday Brisket Dinner with Gravy seems simple to prepare, it is the essence of umami: savory, meaty, and deeply satisfying. Served with mashed potatoes and a pint of stout, it's the perfect restorative after a long week. His Caldo Verde livened with spicy chorizo and leafy kale is a hearty meal, and if your haddock stock is prepared in advance, it can be pulled together quickly for a weeknight supper. This classic soup is a popular dish through the long Maine winters; Chef Clark recommends serving it to loved ones on a cold night.

SUNDAY BRISKET DINNER WITH GRAVY

(SERVES 6–8)

1 whole first-cut brisket, approximately 6–7 pounds
Salt and pepper
Canola oil (or bacon fat, if you prefer)
3 medium onions
1 head garlic
1 bunch fresh thyme
3 tablespoons unsalted butter
3 tablespoons all-purpose flour

Preheat oven to 350°F. Trim brisket of excess fat, leaving some on for flavor. Season both sides of meat with salt and pepper.

In a large Dutch oven, over high heat, sear the brisket in a few tablespoons of canola oil or bacon fat (enough to cover the bottom of the pot) for approximately 6–8 minutes on each side. While brisket is browning, slice onions into ½-inch half moons and separate garlic into individual cloves. When brisket is dark brown on both sides, remove to a holding dish large enough to catch escaping juices.

In the same Dutch oven, add onions, garlic, and thyme. Sauté over high heat until onions begin to brown and the bits of beef left on the bottom of the pot loosen. Put the brisket back into the pot, with its juices, adding enough water to come halfway up the brisket, and cover with the lid. Place in preheated oven. Cook for 3 hours.

When brisket is very tender and pulls apart when tested with a fork, carefully remove the meat from the Dutch oven and place on a plate to rest. Strain the liquid into a bowl, discarding onions, garlic, and thyme. Place Dutch oven back on the stovetop, over medium heat. Add the butter, and when it's melted, whisk in the flour. Let the roux cook until it turns dark brown, whisking often

to keep it from sticking. Add the strained liquid to the brown roux, whisking constantly to avoid lumps. Bring gravy to a simmer and cook for 15 minutes. Season with salt and pepper to taste.

Slice brisket and serve with gravy and your favorite mashed potatoes.

CALDO VERDE

PORTUGUESE KALE & POTATO SOUP WITH CHORIZO

(SERVES 6–8)

2 pounds haddock bones

2 bay leaves

10 peppercorns

3 carrots

3 ribs celery

3 medium onions

2 bunches kale

3 cloves garlic

1 pound fresh chorizo, or ½ pound dried

4 potatoes

Extra virgin olive oil

Salt and pepper

To make the haddock broth: Place the haddock bones in your largest pot with the bay leaves, peppercorns, 1 carrot, and 1 celery rib. Roughly chop 1 onion and add it to the pot. Add enough cold water to cover the ingredients by 1 inch. Bring the pot to a boil, then immediately turn it down to a simmer. (Be careful not to let it boil rapidly, or it will become cloudy.) Simmer broth for 45 minutes, then strain through a cheesecloth or fine strainer. You should have at least 1 quart of haddock stock. The stock can be made a day ahead and refrigerated.

To finish the soup: Finely chop the remaining carrots, celery, and onions, plus the kale and garlic. Peel the potatoes and cut into 1/2-inch cubes. Set aside.

Remove fresh chorizo from casings and crumble. If using dried chorizo, dice finely. Place a sturdy soup pot over medium heat and add enough olive oil to cover the bottom. Add the chorizo and cook until the sausage releases its fat. Add the carrots, celery, onion, and garlic to the pot and let it sweat for 10 minutes. Add the kale and salt and pepper, and sweat for an additional 10 minutes, stirring frequently. Add potatoes and approximately 1 quart of the haddock broth (enough to cover all the ingredients by 1 inch). Simmer until the potatoes are tender, then adjust seasonings to taste.

Caiola's

58 Pine Street
(207) 772-1110
www.caiolas.com
Chef/Owner: Abby Harmon; Co-Owner: Lisa Vaccaro

Open the satisfyingly heavy wooden door to Caiola's, a neighborhood bistro tucked on a quiet side street in the West End, and you immediately notice two things. The first greets you on the cobbled sidewalk: the wafting smell of garlic, onions, and olive oil, staples in a kitchen that's influenced by Chef Abby Harmon's travels in Spain, Italy, and France. The second is the beautifully appointed interior, designed by Chef Harmon's partner Lisa Vaccaro, the restaurant's manager and a woodworker whose aesthetic for the space combines salvaged wood, tile floors, and a changing show of paintings from local artists.

Named for Vaccaro's Italian grandmother, the restaurant serves upscale comfort food, combining Maine native and self-taught Chef Harmon's love of seafood and

local, seasonal ingredients with flavors she's experienced at Vaccaro's family table and abroad. In designing the restaurant, the pair consciously tried to create a casual, comfortable feeling of family celebration. Food is beautiful but not fussy; service is attentive but not overly formal.

The menus, for dinner Tuesday through Saturday and for brunch on Sunday, change regularly, but house favorites include classic Spanish paella, spicy lamb harissa, Spanish rossejat with scallops and shrimp, chicken marsala, and the Caiola's burger, served with bacon, cheddar, and a mound of crisp homemade tater tots. The press has discovered Caiola's, and write-ups have appeared in *Bon Appétit* magazine and the *Washington Post*, but the restaurant has managed to stay refreshingly true to its roots, a neighborhood treat where everyone feels like part of the family.

When cooking the beets for the recipe below, the colors will stay brighter if you boil them with the skins on. For the Wild Mushroom Bruschetta, make sure you begin pickling the black trumpet mushrooms at least half an hour before assembling the dish. If you're unable to grill the bread slices, arrange them on a cookie sheet and toast in a preheated oven at 400°F until crisp.

Wild Mushroom Bruschetta with Pickled Trumpet Mushrooms

(SERVES 6–8)

1 loaf sourdough bread, thinly sliced

1 clove garlic, peeled

Salt and pepper

2 tablespoons olive oil

1 tablespoon minced brown anchovies
(oil-packed, drained)

3 cups cleaned and roughly chopped
wild mushrooms

1 minced shallot

1 tablespoon minced garlic

Freshly squeezed juice of 1 lemon

2 tablespoons unsalted butter

Shaved Parmesan cheese

12 ounces baby spinach, cleaned

Pickled Trumpet Mushrooms (recipe below)

Grill pieces of sourdough bread on both sides. Rub with garlic clove on one side and season with salt and pepper. Set aside until mushrooms are cooked.

In a large heavy-bottomed sauté pan, heat the olive oil over medium-high heat, adding the anchovies and cooking until nutty. Add wild mushrooms, shallot, and garlic, and sauté until mushrooms begin to release their juices. Add lemon juice, butter, and salt and pepper to taste, and cook until flavors are well blended, 3–5 minutes.

To assemble: Top each piece of grilled bread with cooked mushrooms, shaved Parmesan cheese, a few leaves of fresh spinach, and pickled trumpet mushrooms.

PICKLED TRUMPET MUSHROOMS

1 cup black trumpet mushrooms

¼ cup white balsamic vinegar

2 teaspoons honey

salt and pepper to taste

Clean mushrooms well and soak in warm water. While they are soaking, in a small saucepan heat white balsamic vinegar with honey and salt and pepper. Drain mushrooms and place in a small nonreactive bowl. Pour hot vinegar liquid over the mushrooms and let sit for ½ hour before use.

Marinated Beets with Goat Cheese, Poppy Seeds, Arugula, Toasted Nuts & Balsamic Vinegar

(SERVES 4)

9 various beets of similar size (Chioggia, golden, and red), skins on and well scrubbed
¼ cup plus 1 teaspoon dark balsamic vinegar
3 tablespoons honey
Salt and pepper to taste
2 teaspoons minced garlic
1 teaspoon crushed red pepper
1 teaspoon minced ginger
5 tablespoons olive oil
3 oranges
1 red grapefruit
¼ pound arugula or greens of choice
11 ounces creamy goat cheese
1 tablespoon poppy seeds
¼ cup toasted pistachios
½ red onion, thinly sliced

In a large pot over medium-high heat, boil beets until a fork will easily pierce their hearts. Drain and cool beets under cold running water and slip off skins. Quarter beets, place in a large bowl, and set aside.

In a small bowl, mix together ¼ cup balsamic vinegar, honey, salt and pepper, 1 teaspoon minced garlic, crushed red pepper, and ginger. Pour over warm beets, gently stirring to coat. Drizzle beets with 3 tablespoons of the olive oil. Check and adjust; you should taste both the sweet and the tangy, with just a touch of heat from the chilies and warmth from the ginger.

Peel oranges and grapefruit and section into supremes, removing all the white pith from each segment. Set aside.

In a medium-size bowl, toss arugula with remaining 2 tablespoons of olive oil, salt and pepper to taste, and remaining 1 teaspoon of balsamic vinegar. In a separate small bowl, mash together goat cheese and poppy seeds, blending well.

Divide marinated beets between four serving plates. On top of the beets, place a dollop of poppy seed goat cheese, a generous sprinkle of toasted nuts, some thin slices of red onion, the dressed arugula, and supremes of citrus. Just before serving, drizzle marinade from the beets over each plate.

CINQUE TERRE

36 WHARF STREET
(207) 347-6154
WWW.CINQUETERREMAINE.COM
CHEF: LEE SKAWINSKI
OWNERS: DAN KARY AND MICHELLE MAZUR-KARY

A pioneer in the farm-to-table movement, Chef Lee Skawinski's Cinque Terre is a far cry from even the most upscale Italian restaurants. Housed in an old chandlery building on historic Wharf Street, the restaurant serves authentic Italian cuisine, made from local seafood, pasture-raised meats, and vegetables grown on the restaurant's own Grand View Farm in nearby Greene. Absent from the menu are red sauces and alfredos; instead, patrons feast on seared scallops on parsnip puree, roasted duck leg with imported Italian farro and local sautéed kale, hand-cut pasta with pancetta ragù, and the house specialty, Zuppa di Pesce.

An alumnus of Newbury College's Culinary School, Chef Skawinski traveled through Europe after graduation, tasting his way across the Continent while learning about rustic seasonal cooking and top-tier wines before returning to the States to make his culinary name in the kitchens of Boston's Four Seasons Hotel and Freeport's Harraseeket Inn.

Opening Cinque Terre in 2001, he was able to pursue his passion for old-fashioned, ingredient-driven Ligurian cuisine. In the years since the restaurant opened, Chef Skawinski has increasingly grown more of his own produce, and he has received acclaim for his farm-to-table ethos from such varied publications as *GQ, the Washington Post, Gourmet,* and *USA Today.* What isn't local is often imported, and Chef Skawinski makes regular trips to Italy with members of his staff to sample olive oils, vinegars, artisan cheeses and meats, and wines. Twice a presenter at the James Beard House, he's actively involved with the Slow Food movement, and with Gruppo Ristoranti Italiani, a national group dedicated to raising the profile of Italian cuisine.

The Berkshire Pork with Speck, Tuscan Cabbage, and Salsa Verde is a hearty meal with a beautiful presentation. *Speck* and Tuscan ham can be found at Italian grocers, fine markets, and online; for best results, use fresh, organically raised pork tenderloin. Though not normally served in America's Italian restaurants, *cavolo* (cabbage) is one of Italy's most popular winter staples. Cooked until it's nearly caramelized, it takes on a sweetness that's offset by the addition of garlic, ham, and black olives. Any leftovers of the classic Salsa Verde can be paired with other meats, fish, poultry, or grilled or roasted vegetables.

BERKSHIRE PORK WITH SPECK, TUSCAN CABBAGE & SALSA VERDE

(SERVES 4)

For the cabbage:

Olive oil
2 cloves garlic, thinly sliced
¼ cup chopped Tuscan ham
2 leeks, julienned
12 cups sliced green cabbage
40 black olives, chopped

For the pork with speck:

12 slices *speck* (smoked prosciutto)
4 (6-ounce) pieces of pork tenderloin
Small bunch parsley, coarsely chopped
4 cloves garlic, coarsely chopped
Salt and freshly ground black pepper

For the Salsa Verde (Makes 1 quart)

4 bunches parsley, finely chopped
1 teaspoon white balsamic vinegar
2 hard-boiled egg yolks
1 boiled potato, peeled
1 head garlic, cloves peeled and finely chopped
2 white anchovies (also called *alici* or *boquerones*), chopped
3 cups, more or less, extra virgin olive oil
Salt and freshly ground black pepper, to taste

Preheat oven to 400°F.

In a large sauté pan over medium heat, pour in enough olive oil to cover the bottom of the pan. Add sliced garlic and lightly toast. Add Tuscan ham and leeks and sauté for 2 minutes. Add half of the cabbage and sauté for 2 minutes, then stir in the remaining cabbage and chopped black olives. Sauté until the cabbage is completely cooked down and beginning to caramelize. Remove from heat and keep warm until ready to serve.

Lay slices of *speck* flat on a cutting board, side by side. Sprinkle the pork loin with olive oil, parsley, garlic, and salt and pepper. Place each piece of pork on the *speck* and wrap the slices around the loins, so that the *speck* comes to the edge of the meat (you will use 3 pieces of *speck* per loin). Put the meat in a cast iron pan and place it in the preheated oven. Bake for 9 minutes, then turn over and cook for an additional 5 minutes. Remove from oven, place meat on a board and let meat rest for 5 minutes.

To prepare the Salsa Verde: Place parsley, white balsamic vinegar, hard boiled egg yolks, boiled potato, chopped garlic, and chopped white anchovies in a large mixing bowl. Using a balloon whisk, beat vigorously to break down the potato and egg yolks, working until the mixture is well blended. While whisking, start adding olive oil a little at a time until you achieve the desired thickness. The sauce should be spoonable but not runny. Add salt and pepper to taste.

To serve: On each large dinner plate arrange one-quarter of the cabbage in a line. Slice each piece of pork into 4 slices, season with salt and pepper, and place overlapping the cabbage. Spoon Salsa Verde over the top, and drizzle with a good olive oil.

Photos to the right from Cinque Terre's Harvest Dinner at Grandview Farm.

David's Restaurant

22 Monument Square
(207) 773-4425
www.davidsrestaurant.com
Chef/Owner: David Turin

At the edge of Monument Square, under a leafy canopy and a blue neon sign, Chef David Turin's restaurant, David's Restaurant, has been a hub of culinary invention since it opened in 1992. A graduate of Cornell University, Chef Turin began his career as a chef on a charter boat in the Virgin Islands, eventually becoming a licensed boat captain, a scuba diving guide, and an avid surfer.

His culinary career soon took precedence, and since 1983 he's been the chef/owner of nine restaurants in Massachusetts and Maine. With a focus on unusual pairings, Chef Turin's current restaurant has for nearly two decades served dishes that range from classic to experimental. Starters include oysters on the half shell and lobster cakes with

sweet potatoes and red pepper sauce, while entrees like grilled sirloin with roasted garlic mashed potatoes sit on the menu with sushi-rare pepper-crusted tuna with Szechuan citrus dipping sauce and sesame peanut soba noodles.

Loving to experiment in the kitchen, Chef Turin favors meals that give him a challenge. A group of a dozen wine collectors, for example, come to the restaurant several times a year with wines from their own collections, and Chef Turin's challenge—which he embraces wholeheartedly—is to make dishes that pair well with the wines but aren't repeats of earlier meals. Generally the dinners are seven to ten courses, and Chef Turin estimates that he's made at least 120 distinctive dishes for the group, many of which have made it onto the menu at either David's Restaurant or David's 388 (388 Cottage Road, South Portland, 207-347-7388), a small, casual restaurant he opened in 2006.

When making the Duck with Sauternes, Ginger, and Sesame Grilled Iceberg Lettuce, look for Moulard (mulard) or Barbary (Muscovy) duck. The breast meat, or *magret de canard,* is generally large with a lush layer of fat.

Duck with Sauternes, Ginger & Sesame Grilled Iceberg Lettuce

(SERVES 4)

2 duck breasts, approximately 16 ounces each

For the marinade:

1 tablespoon chopped fresh ginger

1½ tablespoons chopped scallions

2 tablespoons chopped garlic

2 tablespoons soy sauce

4 tablespoons sesame oil

3 tablespoons canola oil

For the sauce:

2 tablespoons sugar

½ cup Sauternes

2 tablespoons julienned ginger

2 tablespoons sesame oil

4 wedges iceberg lettuce

Salt and freshly ground black pepper, to taste

Toasted sesame seeds

2 tablespoons soy sauce

2 tablespoons garlic-lemon-herb compound
   butter (see note)

Trim duck breasts and score skin in a crosshatch pattern. Do not cut down as far as the meat.

To make the marinade: In a large bowl, combine ginger, scallions, garlic, soy sauce, and oils. Toss duck breasts in the marinade to coat well, then pour marinade into a shallow dish and place duck breasts, skin side up, in the marinade. Refrigerate overnight.

In a small nonreactive bowl, combine sugar, Sauternes, and julienned ginger, cover, and refrigerate overnight.

The following day, place duck breasts skin side down in a sauté pan over very low heat for 30 minutes to render fat. Make sure that heat is low enough that breasts remain raw. Remove duck breasts from pan and reserve fat.

Before serving, sauté duck breasts skin side down over high heat until fat is fully rendered and skin is crisp. Flip the breasts and sauté until cooked to medium rare. Remove duck breasts to a cutting board, and place skin side up to crisp and rest.

Add sesame oil to duck fat in the sauté pan and sear iceberg wedges until nicely colored. Remove to four serving plates, season with salt and pepper, and strew with toasted sesame seeds.

Add ginger and wine mixture to the pan and cook until mixture is reduced to a syrup. Stir in soy sauce and compound butter to finish. To serve, slice breasts across the grain, arrange on top of the seared lettuce, and drizzle with the ginger sauce.

Note: To make compound butter: In a stand mixer fitted with the paddle attachment, beat together 8 tablespoons (1 stick) unsalted butter, 1 tablespoon chopped fresh parsley, 1 tablespoon freshly squeezed lemon juice, ½ teaspoon salt, and 1–2 pressed cloves of garlic, to taste. When well combined, taste and adjust proportions. Scrape butter mixture onto a large piece of waxed paper, roll into a log, and refrigerate until firm. Compound butter may be frozen for future use.

DUCKFAT

43 MIDDLE STREET
(207) 774-8080
WWW.DUCKFAT.COM
CHEF/OWNER: ROB EVANS; CO-OWNER: NANCY PUGH

In 2004, after being named one of *Food & Wine*'s Top 10 New Chefs for his elegant restaurant Hugo's (page 106), Chef Rob Evans and his wife and business partner Nancy Pugh decided to branch out. Inspired by the abundant local products available in Maine and the desire to have "an approachable space to experiment on fun foods that people love to eat," they created Duckfat, a casual cafe-style restaurant specializing in Belgian duck fat fries, panini stuffed with house-made charcuterie, and milkshakes blended with artisan Maine-made gelato.

Though Chef Evans recalls that a few patrons found the name offensive before they opened, he felt passionately that Duckfat as a name was both descriptive and memorably fun, and in the years they've been open, even the skeptics have come around. How could they not, when presented with a cone of crisp fries, hand cut from Maine potatoes, cooked in duck fat to a perfect golden brown, and served with a choice of aioli, house-made mayonnaise, truffle ketchup, or Eastport's own Raye's Mustard? For the truly decadent, there's poutine, the Canadian classic that here pairs fries with house-made duck gravy and cheese curd from nearby Pineland Farm. Or beignets fried in duck fat and topped with sugar or chocolate sauce, perfect with a cup of locally roasted Coffee By Design, served in a mini French press so you can brew it to your liking.

SPECIALS ⚜

WE SOURCE LOCALLY!

...TINA POTATO w/ VERMONT CHEDDAR $5⁰⁰/CUP $6²⁵/BOWL

...DERELLA PUMPKIN SQUASH, LOCAL
...ED GREENS, TOASTED PUMPKIN SEEDS,
...E CROUTONS w/ A SHERRY VINAIGRETTE $8-

...HN-MI: PORK TWO WAYS (GROUND PORK &
...USE MADE SPAM), PICKLED DAIKON-CARROT
...AW, SRIRACHA-SOY MAYO & CILANTRO $10-

...CKEN LIVER MOUSSE w/ BUTTER CRISP WAFER

...EBERRY-SAGE SODA $2⁵⁰
...MULLED CIDER $1.⁵⁰

DANDELION SPRING FARM
PLAINVIEW FARM
FERN HILL FARM
BECKWITH FARM
PLEASANT HILL FARM
FISHBOWL FARM
UNCLE'S FARMSTAND
MEADOWOOD FARM
SUNSET ACRES FARM
FREEDOM FARM
WALNUT HILL FARM
SNELL FARM
STANDARD BAKING CO.
MORSE'S DELI
RICKER HILL

Customers regularly ask if everything is cooked in duck fat, and the answer is no. There are salads of greens from local farmers, soups "made from scratch and full of lovin'," and panini filled with everything from pork belly to PB&J. Served on ciabatta bread with a cherry pepper mayonnaise, the Pork Belly "BLT" is one of the menu's most popular items. Though it's best in summer when heirloom tomatoes are plentiful, it can be served year round, either omitting the tomatoes or using the best hothouse varieties you can find. As with all cured meats, keep in mind that you need to allow time for brining, in this case 24 hours. At Duckfat, they cure pork belly in large quantities; this will leave you with plenty of leftovers, perfect for serving a crowd, snacking, slicing over greens, adding to sandwiches, or simply experimenting.

PORK BELLY "BLT"

(SERVES 8, WITH LEFTOVERS)

15 pounds pork belly (rind on)

For the pork belly brine:

3 cups sugar
2 cups salt
1½ gallons water
3 cups molasses
1 cup honey
15 whole juniper berries
6 tablespoons roughly ground black peppercorns

For the pork belly rub:

4 tablespoons garlic powder
4 tablespoons onion powder
2 tablespoons marjoram
2 tablespoons paprika
1 tablespoon ground cumin
1 tablespoon instant espresso
1 tablespoon salt
1 tablespoon freshly ground black pepper

For the cherry pepper relish:

3 tablespoons olive oil
4 (7-ounce) jars roasted sweet red peppers,
    rinsed, drained, patted dry, chopped
1½ cups chopped onions
1 tablespoon finely chopped roasted garlic
1 quart pickled cherry peppers, drained
1 (8-ounce) jar banana peppers
4 cups sundried tomatoes
Salt and freshly ground black pepper to taste

Mayonnaise
Sliced ciabatta
Fresh mixed greens
Heirloom tomato slices

Rinse pork belly and pat dry. In a large pot, over medium heat, combine sugar and salt with enough of the water to dissolve them and allow mixture to simmer. When sugar and salt have dissolved, remove from heat and stir in molasses, honey, juniper berries, and the rest of the water. Cool to room temperature. Rub untrimmed pork belly with ground black pepper. Submerge meat in cooled brine, cover, and refrigerate for 24 hours.

Remove pork belly from refrigerator and bring to room temperature (this will take about 1 hour). Combine all ingredients for the pork belly rub in a food processor and pulse for 30 seconds. Set aside.

Place rack in lower third of the oven and preheat to 375°F.

Pat pork dry. Using your hands, smear approximately one-third of the spice rub into all the internal crevices of the pork. With the tip of a knife, puncture the skin, making lots of tiny holes. (This will help the skin become crispy, making a giant crust of "cracklin's" that can be peeled off or eaten. Even if you don't plan to eat the skin, don't remove it before cooking, as it bastes the pork while it's in the oven.) Make some long, shallow slashes in the rest of meat, approximately 2 inches apart and ¼-inch deep, and then rub the remaining herb mixture all over the belly, massaging it into the slashes.

Set the roast, skin side up, in a large roasting pan with no rack. Put the pork in the oven and roast for 20 minutes, then reduce heat to 325°F. Cook for 1 hour more, turning roasting pan occasionally to brown the pork evenly. After 30 minutes, start checking the internal temperature of the meat with a thermometer, continuing to check every 15 minutes until it reaches 140–145°F.

Remove pork belly from the oven and let the meat rest for 30 minutes before carving. To serve, leave the slab whole, slicing meat as it's wanted and reserving pieces of the skin for the "non-fat-afraid."

To make the cherry pepper relish: Combine all ingredients in a food processor and pulse until mixture reaches a coarse consistency.

To assemble each sandwich: Mix 2 tablespoons of mayonnaise with 2 tablespoons of cherry pepper relish and adjust salt and pepper to taste.

Spread the sauce on two slices of ciabatta. Arrange slices of pork belly, mixed greens, and heirloom tomatoes on a slice of ciabatta, topping with the second slice. Grill in a panini press or serve as is.

EAST ENDER

47 MIDDLE STREET
(207) 879-7669
WWW.EASTENDERPORTLAND.COM
CHEF/OWNER: MITCHELL GEROW
CO-OWNER: MEGAN SCHROETER

Serving American comfort food in a two-level storefront with exposed brick, a long mahogany bar, and glimpses of Casco Bay through the trees out front, East Ender has a rustic, almost bucolic feel. Yet its location, tucked at the base of Munjoy Hill in Portland's East End (hence the name), keeps the place bustling with urbanites in search of smoky barbecue, house-pickled corn, and long-simmered Northern Maine beans.

A native of upstate New York, chef/owner Mitchell Gerow draws on a childhood spent hunting, fishing, gardening, and foraging at his parents' side, and an early career studying classic French and Japanese culinary techniques. Now in their own space, Chef Gerow and co-owner Megan Schroeter have crafted a menu that updates patrons' nostalgic memories of childhood, pairing fried bologna sandwiches like grandma used to make with craft beers brewed just miles away. Local meats, fish, fruits, and vegetables are cured, corned, brined, smoked, and pickled in-house, and in addition to barbecue favorites like ribs and brisket, Chef Gerow's repertoire includes less conventional meats like game hens, beef cheeks, and house-made sausages. On weekday mornings the kitchen's fryer is turned over to Leigh Kellis, of the Holy Donut, whose addictive donuts are made with Maine potato flour and range from Buttermilk Maple Walnut to Bacon and Sharp Cheddar.

For his Applewood-Smoked Trout Fritters, Chef Gerow smokes his own fish, beginning with skin-on fillets dusted with his Yellow BBQ Rub. Store any excess rub in a sealed container and use for grilled fish and poultry. If you don't have access to a smoker or a grill, it's fine to use an equal amount of commercially prepared smoked trout. The Lemon Caper Mayonnaise makes enough for a party, but will keep for a week in the refrigerator. Serve leftover sauce with seafood, spread on sandwiches, or as a dip for vegetables.

For its Macaroni and Cheese, East Ender uses a house version of the small, twisted pasta called *trofie.* This is worth making by hand for the rich, yolky flavor it imparts. In a pinch, substitute a high-quality artisan pasta.

APPLEWOOD-SMOKED TROUT FRITTERS
WITH LEMON CAPER MAYONNAISE

(SERVES 6–8)

For the Yellow BBQ Rub:

1 cup ground yellow mustard seed

1 cup ground coriander

2 tablespoons sugar

1 tablespoon onion powder

1 tablespoon turmeric

1 tablespoon crushed red chili peppers

For the smoked trout:

6 trout fillets, skin on

Yellow BBQ Rub, for dusting

Kosher salt and freshly ground black pepper, to taste

½ cup applewood chips

For the fritter batter:

4 eggs, separated

1 cup milk

4 tablespoons cider vinegar

2 tablespoons unsalted butter, melted and cooled

2 cups all-purpose flour

2 teaspoons baking powder

½ teaspoon kosher salt

⅓ cup finely sliced chives

6 cups canola oil, for frying

Lemon Caper Mayonnaise (recipe to the right)

Capers, for garnish

Lemon zest, for garnish

To make the Yellow BBQ Rub: Mix together all the ingredients and place in a sealed jar for storage.

To make the smoked trout: Lightly dust the fish with BBQ rub, kosher salt, and black pepper. In an electric smoker, or over indirect heat on a kettle grill, smoke the trout, skin side down, at 225°F for 20 minutes. Remove from heat and cool to room temperature.

To make the fritter batter: Blend egg yolks, milk, cider vinegar, and melted butter in a large bowl. Sift flour, baking powder, and salt over the bowl, and stir to combine. Cover with plastic wrap and chill for 1 hour. In a separate bowl, whip egg whites until they hold stiff peaks, then fold into the chilled batter. Peel skin from the trout fillets, break fish into small pieces, and mix trout and chives into batter.

In a large pot or deep skillet, heat canola oil to 350°F. Carefully drop tablespoon-sized fritters into the oil (a small thumb-release ice cream scoop works well for this). Agitate fritters as they cook to ensure even browning. Fry until a toothpick inserted in a fritter slides out clean, approximately 4 minutes. Drain cooked fritters briefly on paper towels, sprinkle with salt, and serve piping hot with Lemon Caper Mayonnaise topped with capers and curls of lemon zest.

LEMON CAPER MAYONNAISE

(MAKES 6 CUPS)

1 whole egg
2 egg yolks
1 tablespoon Dijon mustard
1 tablespoon champagne vinegar
1 tablespoon simple syrup (see note on page 34)
Juice of ½ lemon
4 cups canola oil
Splash of cold water
Zest of 1 lemon
Pickled nonpareil capers, to taste

In the bowl of a food processor, combine egg
and yolks, mustard, vinegar, simple syrup, and
lemon juice. With the blade whirring, slowly add
oil in a thin stream, processing until mayonnaise is
emulsified. Blend in a splash of cold water to set
the mayonnaise. Scrape sauce into a medium size
bowl and stir in lemon zest and capers, to taste.

Macaroni & Cheese

(SERVES 6–8)

For the pasta (trofie):

1¾ cups all-purpose flour, plus more
    for kneading
6 egg yolks
1 whole egg
Splash of extra virgin olive oil
Splash of milk

For the cheese sauce:

2 tablespoons plus 1 teaspoon unsalted butter
½ medium white onion, minced
2 tablespoons all-purpose flour
Splash of white wine
4 cups whole milk
1½ cups grated aged cheddar cheese
Dash of grated nutmeg
Kosher salt and freshly ground black pepper, to taste
1 tablespoon finely chopped parsley
1 tablespoon finely sliced chives
Pinch of paprika
Toasted bread crumbs

To make the pasta: Sift flour into a large bowl. Make a well in the center of the flour and add egg yolks, egg, oil, and milk. Using your fingers, slowly mix in flour from the edges, kneading to make a stiff dough. Lightly flour a smooth work surface and turn out the dough, pushing it and kneading with the heels of your hands for 15 minutes. The dough will become silky and elastic as you knead. Gather into a ball and cover with plastic wrap, then refrigerate for 30 minutes.

Take out of the refrigerator, remove plastic wrap, and use a rolling pin, pasta roller, or wine bottle to roll out dough to ⅛-inch thickness. Cut with a sharp knife into 1-inch ribbons, then cut each ribbon into ¼-inch-wide rectangles. With your thumb, roll the rectangles one at a time into twists (*trofie*). Set aside finished twists and let stand, uncovered, until firm and sturdy.

When ready to cook, bring a large pot of salted water to a rapid boil (proportions should be roughly 4 cups of water to 1 cup of pasta). Add *trofie* and boil until tender (start testing for doneness after 3 minutes). Drain in a colander, and let stand. Do not rinse.

To make the cheese sauce: Melt 1 teaspoon butter in a large pot over low heat. Add onion and sauté until translucent but not browned. Add remaining 2 tablespoons butter to the pot, and once it is melted, stir in flour with a wooden spoon, sautéing until flour is golden. Pour in a splash of wine, stir to incorporate, and simmer for 1 minute. Gradually add the milk, stirring continuously with a stiff whisk. Bring to a simmer and, still whisking, slowly add the grated cheese. Return to a simmer and season with nutmeg, salt, and pepper. Pass mixture through a fine strainer, then return to the pot, bring to a simmer, and add *trofie* to the sauce. Continue to simmer, stirring in parsley and chives. Pour into a serving dish and top with paprika and bread crumbs before serving.

CRAFT BREWS— BEER AND BEYOND

Maine brewers have been crafting artisan ales for decades, and their goods can be sampled on the **Maine Beer Trail,** a guided map of the best brewpubs and microbreweries around the state (www.mainebrewersguild.org). In the past few years, another crop of brewers has sprouted up: mead makers and cider fermenters. Working with ingredients that are native to Maine, craft meads and hard ciders are making a splash on the culinary scene. Businesses like **Maine Mead Works** (51 Washington Avenue; 207-773-6323) and the **Urban Farm Fermentory** (200 Anderson Street, Bay 4; 207-653-7406) are based in Portland's East End, and are turning out tasty brews with a light fizz and a little kick. Made from local honey and apples, both mead and cider are drier than you'd expect, making them a refreshing alternative to beer and wine. Look for them by the bottle and on menus around town or, better yet, take a tour of one of the fermentories and stop by the tasting room.

El Rayo Taqueria

101 York Street
(207) 780-8226
WWW.ELRAYOTAQUERIA.COM
Chef: Cheryl Lewis

When Chef Cheryl Lewis had her first taco, at age six in the house of a neighbor in upstate New York, it was love at first bite. Though she learned to cook at her mother's side, preparing "ladies' luncheons from the Craig Claiborne column in the *New York Times*," Lewis vividly remembers her introduction to the warm spices of Mexico, both at her neighbor's and on trips to visit family in California—during which she invariably sought out taco stands. Decades later, after years of operating restaurants and cafes on both coasts with her business and life partner, Noreen Kotts, Lewis brought her craving for fresh, authentic Mexican food to her adopted home of Portland.

In a brightly painted converted gas station on a busy corner near the waterfront, Lewis and Kotts originally envisioned El Rayo as a *taquería* selling tacos and cheese-covered grilled corn on a strictly take-out basis. Their popularity quickly outstripped this model, and the couple used their thirty years of restaurant experience to creatively reimagine the space. Now El Rayo Taqueria has table service at indoor and outdoor seating, an expanded menu that ranges from smoky potato fritters with chipotle sauce to ceviche and ever-popular fish tacos, and regular live music (local bands, not mariachi). Across the parking lot, the recently opened El Rayo Cantina has a more subdued feel, and is open later with a more refined menu of small plates and an expanded list of cocktails. At both restaurants, the commitment to local sourcing and chef-driven

food is clear: nothing is jarred or canned, and the kitchen staff spends each morning roasting, grilling, and marinating ingredients, including preserving their own locally grown jalapeños. Lewis and Kotts are proud that the core team that helped open El Rayo in 2009 continues to work there—they all consider it a family business. And Lewis has also earned her long-ago neighbor's seal of approval: the tortilla press used to make that first taco now hangs in her kitchen.

A riff on Oysters Rockefeller that combines the flavors of New England and Mexico, Nonesuch Oysters with Chili Pesto are a favorite at El Rayo. As Chef Lewis enthuses, "We adore the briny luscious oysters from Nonesuch Oyster Farm in Pine Point. Abigail Carroll has carefully nursed these oysters along, and now the restaurants in Portland are all vying for a share!" If you're lucky enough to find them, try making this recipe with Nonesuch, but if you're cooking across state lines, choose a rich, briny oyster that will stand up to spices in the pesto.

For the Mexico City Style Roasted Corn, rolled in Chipotle Mayonnaise and grated Cotija cheese, make sure the corn is plump and fresh, and don't shuck it in advance. You'll have leftover Chipotle Mayonnaise, but it's so addictive that you'll find yourself spreading it on everything from sandwiches to chicken breast. As a substitute for plain mayonnaise, it can also add a Southwestern touch to deviled eggs, potato salad, and the like. Cotija cheese, a firm white cow's milk cheese popular in Mexican cooking, can be found in Mexican markets and in the Mexican section of better groceries. If you can't find it, substitute Parmesan—the flavor won't be quite the same, but it will add the cheese's sharp kick.

NONESUCH OYSTERS WITH CHILI PESTO

(SERVES 6–8)

3 whole poblano peppers
1 whole green pepper
1 teaspoon minced garlic
2 ounces Cotija cheese, grated
½ cup pumpkin seeds
¼ cup packed parsley leaves
2 tablespoons canola oil
Salt to taste

4 dozen oysters
1 cup bread crumbs

On a grill or under the broiler, roast poblano and green peppers, scorching all surfaces. Place hot peppers in a bowl, cover with plastic, and allow to steam for 10 minutes.

Working over the bowl, peel and seed peppers, catching any juice to add to the pesto. To maximize the flavor, be careful not to rinse peppers with water.

Place peppers and their juices, garlic, cheese, pumpkin seeds, parsley, and canola oil in the bowl of a food processor and blend until smooth. Add salt to taste.

To serve: Shuck the oysters, leaving the oyster in the deeper half of the shell and being careful to cut the muscle underneath. Spread 2 teaspoons of pesto in a thin layer on each oyster and top with a scattering of bread crumbs. Place oysters under the broiler until pesto is bubbling and bread crumbs are golden brown. Serve warm.

OYSTERS

Mollusks, crustaceans, and all kinds of fish thrive in the cold waters off the rocky coast of Maine, and all along the coast conditions are ideal for the cultivation of oysters. The character of the oysters—the crisp, meaty Little Bays harvested near Eliot in the south, the dense, briny Glidden Points found in the deep waters at the mouth of the mid-coast Damariscotta River, the deep-cupped, metallic Taunton Bays found near northern Acadia Park—are shaped by the waters in which they've grown. Though some oysters are exported beyond state lines, the majority are from small producers who harvest just enough to tantalize gourmands around Maine. For a guided tasting of the season's best, stop by one of Portland's many raw bars, from the elegant Old Port Sea Grill (page 123) to the casual J's Oyster Bar, which juts out on a pier overlooking the working waterfront.

Mexico City Style Roasted Corn with Chipotle Mayonnaise

(SERVES 6–8)

12 ears of corn, husks on
Canola oil
Chipotle mayonnaise, for serving (recipe below)
Grated Cotija cheese, for serving

In a sink or deep pot, soak the corn, husks and all, in cold water for 1 hour. Weight the corn with a pot lid or plate to make sure the ears are completely submerged.

While corn is soaking, preheat oven to 400°F. Remove corn from water, leaving husks on, and place in a large roasting pan. Roast for 45 minutes. Remove from oven and let cool enough to handle. Peel away the husks, making sure to keep the stalk or "handle" attached. (The preparation to this point can be done a day in advance; just refrigerate the corn until ready to use.)

Lightly oil each ear of corn and place on a hot grill, roasting until the corn is lightly charred on all sides. While still hot, baste corn heavily with Chipotle Mayonnaise, using a pastry brush to coat evenly. Roll the basted corn in grated Cotija cheese and serve hot.

CHIPOTLE MAYONNAISE

1 tablespoon chopped garlic
¼ cup chipotle chilies in adobo
½ ounce fresh cilantro, chopped
¾ teaspoon Boyajian lime oil, or 2 teaspoons lime zest
2 tablespoons freshly squeezed lime juice
2 cups mayonnaise

Puree all ingredients except mayonnaise in a food processor or blender until very smooth. Add the mayonnaise and blend just until thoroughly mixed. Taste for salt and adjust the balance of ingredients to your preference.

Emilitsa

547 Congress Street
(207) 221-0245
WWW.EMILITSA.COM
Chef/Owner: Demos Regas; Co-Owner: John Regas

Beneath a stylized swinging metal sign that reads simply "E," brothers John and Demos Regas have brought the Greek concept of *philoxenia,* taking care of strangers, to Portland in the form of Emilitsa Estiatorio, their contemporary Greek restaurant on Congress Street. Growing up in the Midwest above Cafe Regas, their family's restaurant, the brothers were raised "with flavorful food and the proverbial welcome mat, whether in our father's restaurant or our mother's kitchen." At the restaurant, their father served patrons American comfort food, while upstairs in the family's home, visitors were treated to their mother's traditional Greek cuisine, richly flavored and prepared, as the brothers do today, with the best and freshest ingredients. "Carpenter, salesman, neighbor or cousin, all were offered a bite of baklava or a sip of Metaxa," Demos recalls.

Since childhood the brothers have had preferred roles in the restaurant: Eight-year-old John greeted customers and served coffee, while Demos stayed in the kitchen, peeling potatoes for a penny apiece and watching their father cook. Today at Emilitsa, John's easy charm welcomes guests in the front of the house, while Demos and his youngest son, Niko, prep, grill, and sauce in the back. The restaurant is named for their mother, and the menu is filled with her recipes—handed down through generations

and shaped by Demos's careful palate (in addition to learning at his mother's side, he spent time at New York's Culinary Institute of America). From marinated lamb chops to savory moussaka, dishes are true to their Greek roots, and, continuing in the tradition of *philoxenia,* all guests are greeted with a simple, perfectly seasoned dal lentil spread on warm homemade bread. The brothers note that the bread is similar to a recipe Emilitsa would prepare on Saturday evenings for the week ahead, giving slices fresh from the oven to her children when they finished bathing in preparation for church the next morning.

A commitment to using seasonal ingredients can be tricky when cooking Mediterranean food in Maine, but the Regas brothers have formed strong relationships with farmers and purveyors throughout the state, and Demos chooses seasonal greens, farm-fresh pork loin, and whole fish from the day's catch to pair with the briny olives and pungent oregano that are essential to Greek cuisine. The exclusively Greek wine list has evolved over the years, and now includes bottles rarely found outside Greece. The brothers buy the best as a tribute to their mother. "Emilitsa would have chosen nothing less for her guests."

Emilitsa's classic moussaka is a favorite among patrons; when it was briefly removed from the menu, there was an uproar. The rich tomato sauce can be made ahead and kept refrigerated, and leftover sauce can be tossed with pasta. The recipe for delicate,

succulent Daurade in Latholemono Sauce comes straight from the island of Évvoia, Emilitsa Regas's birthplace. Note that the recipe calls for whole *daurade royale* or sea bream, which must be scaled and gutted as soon as possible, so you may want to arrange in advance with your local fishmonger. Any leftover Latholemono Sauce can be jarred and stored in the refrigerator for use as a salad dressing or vegetable dip. If it separates, simply pulse again in the blender.

EMILITSA'S MOUSSAKA
(SERVES 8–12)

6 medium-size young eggplant
Extra virgin olive oil
Salt and freshly ground pepper
4 tablespoons butter
4 cups finely chopped Spanish onion
5 cloves garlic, minced
2½ pounds ground beef (85 percent lean)
½ cup finely chopped flat-leaf parsley
½ teaspoon dried Greek oregano
2 cinnamon sticks
1½ teaspoons ground cinnamon, or more to taste
2 tablespoons sugar
2 cups Basic Tomato Sauce (recipe on next page)
2 cup dry white wine, such as Assyrtiko
4 ounces tomato paste, if needed, to thicken
4 cups Yogurt Bechamel Sauce (recipe on next page)
2½ cups grated Parmesan cheese

Preheat oven to 425°F. Cut eggplant crosswise to form rounds ½ inch thick. Place on lightly oiled sheet pans and brush generously with extra virgin olive oil. Sprinkle lightly with salt and pepper. Bake for 18 minutes or until tender. When finished, loosen the eggplant from bottom of pans and set aside to cool.

In a large skillet over medium-high heat melt the 4 tablespoons of butter. Add the onion, garlic, and ground beef, and sauté until the beef is evenly browned, breaking it up with a fork until it is cooked. Salt and pepper to taste. Add parsley, oregano, cinnamon sticks, ground cinnamon, sugar, and tomato sauce. Stir to mix well and let simmer for 2 minutes. Add wine and simmer uncovered until liquid is reduced and mixture has thickened, about 20–30 minutes. The mixture should have the texture of a sloppy joe. If it's too thin, use a little tomato paste to thicken. If it's too thick, use more wine to thin it out. When finished, remove from heat and set aside.

While the beef mixture is simmering, prepare the Yogurt Bechamel Sauce.

Preheat oven to 350° F. Lightly oil a deep 9 x 13-inch baking pan. Layer half the eggplant on the bottom of the pan, trying not to leave any space open. Sprinkle eggplant layer with Parmesan cheese. Spoon on all the beef mixture and sprinkle with more Parmesan cheese. Cover the beef mixture with the remaining eggplant and one more layer of Parmesan cheese. Finish the top layer with the bechamel sauce and generously sprinkle more Parmesan cheese to finish. Bake on middle rack of oven for 30–45 minutes or until cheese is golden brown. Remove from oven, set aside to cool for 10 minutes, then cut into 3-inch squares and plate.

TOMATO SAUCE

(MAKES APPROXIMATELY 4 CUPS)

¾ cup extra virgin olive oil
1 large Spanish onion, chopped
3 cloves garlic, minced
4 pounds ripe plum tomatoes, peeled, seeded, and chopped
2 tablespoons sugar
2 bay leaves
1 tablespoon dried Greek oregano
Salt and pepper to taste

Warm olive oil in a large saucepan over medium-high heat. Add the onion and garlic, and sweat until translucent. Add tomatoes, sugar, bay leaf, and oregano. Stir and bring to a simmer. Turn burner down and continue a low simmer uncovered for about 1 hour or until sauce thickens, stirring occasionally. Remove bay leaves and season with salt and pepper to taste. While still warm, force through a food mill to finish the sauce. Cool and refrigerate up to 5 days.

YOGURT BECHAMEL SAUCE

(MAKES APPROXIMATELY 4 CUPS)

4 cups whole milk
8 tablespoons (1 stick) butter
8 tablespoons all-purpose flour
1 teaspoon onion powder
Freshly grated nutmeg to taste
Very small pinch of ground cloves
⅛ teaspoon freshly ground white pepper
¼ cup grated Parmesan cheese
¼ cup Greek yogurt
6 egg yolks

In a heavy saucepan over medium heat, bring the milk to a simmer. Remove from heat and set aside.

While milk is warming, make a roux. In a sauté pan melt butter over medium heat. Gradually whisk the flour into the butter and cook for a full 3 minutes, whisking continuously and being careful that the mixture does not color. Next, slowly whisk the roux into the heated milk. Put the saucepan of milk back on the burner at medium-low heat. Continue whisking constantly while adding the onion powder, nutmeg, ground cloves, and white pepper. Increase heat a little and cook for 5 minutes, whisking the whole while as the sauce thickens, being careful not to scorch the milk.

When thickened, remove from heat. In a small bowl, lightly beat the egg yolks. Stirring continuously, add ½ cup of the hot sauce to the yolks, then whisk the yolk mixture into the sauce. Put the saucepan back on the burner over medium heat, and continue to whisk until the milk starts to simmer. When thick, remove from heat and fold in the Parmesan cheese, then set aside. When sauce has cooled, fold in the yogurt and set aside until ready to use.

Tsipoúra tis Skaras

DAURADE IN LATHOLEMONO SAUCE

(MAKES 2 GENEROUS SERVINGS)

2 fresh *daurade royale* or sea bream,
    about 1½ pounds each
Freshly squeezed lemon juice
1 small lemon
6 garlic cloves, peeled
Sea salt and freshly cracked black pepper
1 small bunch fresh thyme
1 small bunch fresh rosemary

1 small bunch fresh parsley (optional)
1 small zucchini, sliced into ¼-inch
    diagonal slices
1 small yellow squash, sliced into ¼-inch
    diagonal slices
Extra virgin olive oil
1 pound rainbow chard
1 batch Latholemono Sauce (recipe on next page)

Start your grill and let charcoal burn until white. The grill must be very hot. Indoors, preheat oven to 425°F at the same time.

Leaving scaled fish whole, with the heads and tails on, wipe down body and cavity with lemon juice and cold water. Pat dry.

Slice lemon into ⅛-inch rounds and roughly chop the garlic. Open the cavity of each fish and sprinkle lightly with salt and pepper. Inside each fish, place half the garlic, then line one side of the cavity with half the lemon rounds and top with 3 or 4 sprigs of both thyme and rosemary and a few sprigs of fresh parsley (if using), placed lengthwise on top of the lemon rounds.

Place the fish on the heated grill to char the skin. There's no need to brush the fish with olive oil, as the skin of the daurade will give off plenty of its own tasty oil as it grills. When it starts to sweat its oil, sprinkle a little sea salt and cracked pepper over the skin. Grill the fish 3–4 minutes on each side, or until the skin is crisp and golden brown, or the edges of the fins begin to burn. Keep in mind that you're only grill-marking and browning the fish at this point—it will finish baking in the oven.

When skin is crisped, arrange the fish in a nonreactive pan or tray and place in the preheated oven. Bake for 6–9 minutes, depending on the weight. Test fish for doneness with a metal cake tester or needle by inserting it into the thickest portion of the flesh (usually near the dorsal fin on the fish's back). Hold needle in flesh for 8 seconds and quickly remove and place needle on your chin or lower lip. If the needle is warm to the touch, fish is done. If needle is cool at all, or room temperature, fish needs more time in the oven.

While fish is grilling, brush zucchini and yellow squash with olive oil and place on the hot grill to mark both sides. Remove from grill when marked, sprinkle with sea salt and cracked pepper, and place on baking tray to finish in the oven.

While fish and vegetables are baking, rinse rainbow chard with cold water and pat dry. Strip leaves from the middle vein and discard stem. Just before serving, heat 3 tablespoons olive oil in a large sauté pan over high heat. When oil is almost at the smoking point, drop chard into the pan, adding a dash of sea salt and cracked pepper to taste. Quickly toss with tongs until chard just begins to wilt, then remove from pan and arrange on two serving plates. The chard will form a bed for the fish.

To serve: Place the finished daurade on top of the sautéed chard and arrange slices of each squash next to the fish. Drizzle lightly with olive oil and a pinch of sea salt. Drizzle a fair amount of Latholemono Sauce over the fish, and garnish with a couple sprigs of thyme, stemming from the gills, and half a lemon next to (not on) the fish.

LATHOLEMONO SAUCE

1 cup extra virgin olive oil, unfiltered if possible
3 cloves garlic, peeled and minced
¼ teaspoon Mediterranean sea salt
¼ cup fresh squeezed lemon juice

To make the sauce: Place all ingredients in a robot coupe or blender and pulse until emulsion is formed. The sauce should be somewhat creamy. If you make it in advance and the sauce begins to separate, simply re-pulse to emulsify.

THE FARMER'S TABLE

205 COMMERCIAL STREET
(207) 347-7479
WWW.FARMERSTABLEMAINE.COM
CHEF/OWNER: JEFF LANDRY

With a background both in kitchens and on farms, it's only natural that the inspiration for Chef Jeff Landry's Old Port restaurant, the Farmer's Table, would come from the fields. After six years operating an organic farm, Chef Landry opened the Farmer's Table in 2009 with the motto "You don't need a lot of ingredients. Just the right ones." This philosophy is put into effect in his Mediterranean farmhouse menu, which focuses on showcasing the flavors of Maine. A cheerful and effusive presence, "Chef Jeff" and his sous-chef Michael Rivera prepare simple dishes that can range from homemade pasta with olive oil, garlic, and cheese to house favorite balsamic-braised beef shortribs served over soft polenta. A member of the Maine Organic Farmers and Gardeners' Association, Chef Landry and the restaurant have been recognized by the World Society for the Protection of Animals for a commitment to sourcing humanely raised meats, poultry, and eggs, and Chef Landry has a relationship with all his suppliers; he's been known to swing by his neighbor's farm to pick up the day's produce on his way to work.

The restaurant itself, housed in a service station that was converted to a restaurant space in the late 1980s, is intimate, with a curved outer wall and seating that doubles when weather allows the upper and lower patios to open. From the upstairs, patrons

can watch tankers and cruise ships navigate the islands of Casco Bay, but Chef Landry's excitement comes from his proximity to the working waterfront. Watching an enormous boat glide by, he says, "I love being so close to the water, but I'm glad I don't have to steer that!"

Of the restaurant's ratatouille, Chef Landry notes, "When your garden starts producing more zucchini and summer squash than you can use, ratatouille is a better alternative to using zucchini for bread and baseball bats. It's a pure concentration of summer flavors, accented with plenty of extra virgin olive oil. Since this recipe is all done on the stovetop, I'd highly recommend serving it with grilled fish or meat to add another layer of flavor to the finished dish."

As a native Mainer, Chef Landry is thrilled to use two of Maine's most iconic ingredients, lobsters and potatoes, in his summer classic, Maine Lobster, Lemon Gnocchi, Brown Butter, and Summer Salad. His preferred salad includes greens, snap peas, zucchini, and "whatever else is ripe in the garden." If you can't find fresh lobster, shrimp or lump crab can be substituted. Most important, "Keep the vegetables light, raw and crisp to offset the softer textures of other ingredients, and really try to make your own gnocchi. Not only will it taste better, but you made gnocchi! Well done!"

Ratatouille

(MAKES 8 SERVINGS, AS AN APPETIZER OR SIDE DISH)

1½ cups extra virgin olive oil

2 cups finely diced red onion

3 tablespoons minced fresh garlic

2 cups finely diced eggplant

2 cups finely diced zucchini

2 cups finely diced yellow squash

3 tablespoons tomato paste

2 tablespoons chopped fresh oregano

In a pot large enough to hold all ingredients comfortably, heat olive oil over medium-high heat. Lightly sauté the onions with the garlic, and as the garlic turns golden—not brown—add the eggplant, zucchini, and yellow squash. Sauté for 5 minutes, until squash begins to color. Add the tomato paste, and stir well to incorporate. Reduce heat to low, stir in the oregano, and let simmer uncovered for 30 minutes, stirring occasionally to check for any sticking. If the low setting on your stove is too low to maintain a simmer, turn up the heat a bit. While cooking, it may seem like there is a lot of olive oil, but it is intensely flavored, so use it as part of the sauce for accompanying fish or meat, or spoon out some oil and serve it with bread.

MAINE LOBSTER, LEMON GNOCCHI, BROWN BUTTER & SUMMER SALAD

(MAKES 8 APPETIZER SERVINGS, OR 4 ENTREES)

For the gnocchi:

1 pound large, floury white potatoes
  (not a waxy variety like Yukon Gold)
Zest of 2 lemons
2 cups all-purpose flour, sifted
8 ounces unsalted butter, cut into small cubes

For the lobster:

4 live Maine lobsters, each about 1¼ pounds
Salt and freshly ground black pepper, to taste

For the salad:

2 cups mixed greens (arugula, spinach, mesclun)
3 cups assorted summer vegetables, cut into
  julienne or small bites
¼ cup vinaigrette (red wine vinaigrette preferred)

To make the gnocchi: Place potatoes with skins on in a large pot over medium-high heat and boil until a knife easily pierces them. Remove from the pot and let cool for 10 minutes. Remove skins, being careful, as potatoes will still be hot. Pass potatoes through a food mill or potato ricer into a large mixing bowl. (If you don't own a food mill or potato ricer, use a potato masher and mash as well as possible. Don't use an electric mixer, as this will cause the potatoes to become starchy and gluey.)

Add the lemon zest and flour to the bowl and, using your hands, begin to incorporate. Mixing as little as possible, combine the ingredients and knead lightly. Cut off pieces of the dough and on a well-floured surface roll dough into ½-inch-thick ropes. Using a sharp knife, cut each rope of dough into ½-inch pieces.

Line a pan that will fit in your freezer (jelly roll pans are perfect) with wax paper or parchment and place pieces of dough on the pan as you work. If the gnocchi is sticky, add a little more flour as you roll. Freeze the gnocchi thoroughly. (Gnocchi preparation can be done up to 3 days in advance.)

To cook the lobster: Fill a large pot halfway with salted water. Cover and bring to a boil. Add live lobsters to the pot, one at a time, being careful not to splash yourself with scalding water. Cook lobsters until they turn red, 10–12 minutes. Remove lobsters from the hot water and let cool for 10 minutes on the counter, then an additional 15 minutes in the refrigerator. (If you are substituting crabmeat or shrimp, skip this step. If using uncooked shrimp, cook shrimp until firm and pink in a well-seasoned boil of salted water, peppercorns, lemon, and bay leaf.) When cool enough to handle, remove meat from the shells (or peel and devein shrimp) and cut into bite-size pieces.

To assemble the dish: Bring a large pot of salted water to a boil. While water is coming to a boil, place a large nonstick pan over medium-high heat and melt the butter. Drop the frozen gnocchi into boiling water and cook until they rise to the surface and float for 1 minute. Strain in a colander and gently pour the gnocchi into the pan of melted butter, letting them brown lightly. Add the lobster (or shrimp or crabmeat) to the pan and let it heat through, then season to taste with salt and pepper. The butter should have taken on a brown color—not black or light golden—and should smell nutty.

To serve: Divide the gnocchi and lobster evenly among plates or shallow bowls. Mix the greens and vegetables thoroughly with the vinaigrette and top each dish with the salad. Serve immediately.

THE "OLD PORT"

Now a charming district of cobbled streets, sweet boutiques, and delicious restaurants, the Old Port was at one time the working waterfront of Portland, a warren of winding streets between industrial warehouses, lapped by the waters of Casco Bay. In the center of the city's original peninsula, the buildings of the Old Port once stopped at Fore Street, with what's currently Wharf Street marking the waterfront at high tide. In 1850 the longer and wider Commercial Street was laid out and filled in, and since then it's served as the edge of Portland's dry land. The Old Port district suffered the most damage during the Great Fire of 1866, but it was rebuilt to include many spectacular specimens of architecture from that period, preserved and visible on walking tours of the area. Following decades of neglect, the Old Port began a renaissance in the 1970s, when developers began renovating the area's historic buildings for residential and commercial use. Currently the district is the heart of Portland's tourism industry, and home to many of the city's greatest historical attractions and finest restaurants.

Figa

249 Congress Street
(207) 518-9400
www.figarestaurant.com
Chef/Owner: Lee Farrington

When chef/owner Lee Farrington's hair stylist closed her shop to join the Peace Corps, Farrington saw it as an opportunity. She'd been looking for a space for more than two years, and over dinner she decided to buy the building and open Figa, her globally inspired restaurant at the base of Munjoy Hill. Named for a sixteenth-century Brazilian good luck symbol, Figa is an homage to Farrington's family—her mother is from Brazil—and also a sign of the serendipity that brought the restaurant into being. Having studied at the French Culinary Institute in Manhattan, Farrington cooked both traditional French cuisine at New York's Balthazar and French-Indian at Danny Meyer's now defunct Tabla, but found a different culinary climate when she moved to Maine seven years ago. Cooking at several restaurants in Portland, Farrington watched the culinary scene shift over the years, and in 2010 she opened the much anticipated Figa. Farrington's focus is on spices—roasted, toasted, and ground—and her menu is arranged into "spoons," "forks," and "knives," which roughly translate into small tastes, half portions, and large portions. Wild Boar Rendang and Sev Scallops are among the most popular items on

the changing menu, which nods to Asia and South America, while incorporating local cheeses, meats, and seasonal vegetables.

A long-simmering braise, *rendang* has its roots in Indonesia, where it refers to a dish made with meat stewed in coconut milk and spices. Figa's Wild Boar Rendang cooks for up to five hours, perfuming the kitchen with exotic spice. If your butcher can't find wild boar, you can substitute beef shoulder, though the dish will miss its gamy undertones. Jaggery, an unrefined sugar used in Indian cooking, is available at most Asian markets. If you can't find it, brown sugar can be substituted. *Sev,* a crispy vermicelli-like snack food made of chickpea flour, is also known as *omapodi* and *karapusa*, and is available at Indian markets.

WILD BOAR RENDANG WITH COCONUT RICE

(SERVES 8)

2 cups shredded unsweetened coconut

5 whole shallots, peeled

3 cloves garlic

15 dried chilies

2-inch piece ginger root

5 stalks lemongrass, chopped into 1-inch pieces

2 teaspoons coriander seed

2 teaspoons fennel seed

2 teaspoons cumin seed

Pinch of nutmeg

1 boar shoulder, 3–4 pounds, boned, cut into
    2–3-inch chunks, any silver skin removed

Salt and freshly ground pepper

Vegetable oil

2 tablespoons jaggery

5 cloves

3-inch cinnamon stick

2 (12-ounce) cans unsweetened coconut milk

4 (12-ounce) cans stewed tomatoes, pureed in blender

1 cup water

Coconut Rice (recipe on next page)

Watercress

Extra virgin olive oil and balsamic vinegar, to taste

Preheat oven to 350°F. Spread shredded coconut on a large cookie sheet and toast until golden brown and fragrant, about 10 minutes. Set aside to cool.

Using a blender or food processor, chop shallots, garlic, chilies, ginger, and lemongrass, processing until they make a smooth paste. In a mortar and pestle or electric spice grinder, grind together coriander, fennel, cumin, and nutmeg.

Preheat oven to 350°F. Rinse and pat dry the meat, then sprinkle with salt and pepper.

In a large Dutch oven, heat a splash of vegetable oil over medium-high heat. Add shallot paste and ground spices and cook 2–3 minutes, stirring constantly. Add the meat to the pan, stirring to brown and coat with spices. Stir in jaggery, toasted coconut, cloves, cinnamon stick, coconut milk, pureed tomatoes, and water, and bring to a boil. Cover and place in oven, cooking at a slow braise for 3–5 hours, until meat is meltingly tender.

Serve with unsweetened coconut rice and a handful of watercress drizzled with olive oil and balsamic vinegar.

COCONUT RICE

(SERVES 8)

2 cups Arborio rice
3 (12-ounce) cans unsweetened coconut milk
3 cups water (swirled in the empty coconut milk cans)
Pinch of salt
½ cup unsweetened coconut flakes

In a heavy, large pot over low heat, combine all ingredients and simmer until rice is tender, about 45 minutes. Serve warm.

SEV SCALLOPS WITH JICAMA APPLE PEAR SLAW

(SERVES 4)

1 apple

1 pear

1 small jicama

2 tablespoons rice wine vinegar

3 tablespoons extra virgin olive oil

2 tablespoons plain yogurt

1 teaspoon ground cumin

1 tablespoon curry powder

1 teaspoon honey

Salt, to taste

1 pound diver scallops

Salt and freshly ground black pepper, to taste

1 8-ounce package *sev*

2 tablespoons vegetable oil

1 tablespoon butter

To make the slaw: Julienne the apple, pear, and jicama, and toss to combine. Set aside. To make the vinaigrette, mix together the rice wine vinegar, olive oil, yogurt, cumin, curry powder, and honey, making sure to blend thoroughly. Add salt to taste. Set aside.

To make the scallops: Rinse and pat dry, making sure to remove the white membrane from each scallop. Gently crumble the *sev*, so it's in small pieces that will adhere to the scallops. Season scallops with salt and pepper, then toss them in *sev* to coat.

In a large skillet over medium-high heat, heat the oil and butter until butter has melted and foam has subsided. Cook the *sev*-coated scallops until browned on each side. Cook scallops to your preferred doneness—if you like them with a soft, buttery center, this will be less than 1 minute on each side; if you prefer a firmer scallop, this may be 1½ to 2 minutes per side.

To serve: Place a mound of slaw in the middle of each plate and arrange scallops on each side. Drizzle the plate and slaw with vinaigrette, and serve while scallops are warm.

Five Fifty-Five

555 Congress Street
(207) 761-0555
www.fivefifty-five.com
Chef/Owner: Steve Corry; Co-Owner: Michelle Corry

In the early years of Five Fifty-Five, chef/owner Steve Corry would roll a wagon down Congress Street to the Monument Square farmers' market, fill it with the best-looking vegetables he could find, and create each day's menu accordingly. Though his roots and culinary education were in New England, Chef Corry spent many years in Northern California, first as a brewmaster and later in the kitchen of Napa Valley's famed Domaine Chandon. With his wife, Michelle, whose career has included time at the renowned French Laundry in California and at Arrows in Ogunquit, Chef Corry moved back to

Maine to work at the White Barn Inn, and in 2003 the couple opened Five Fifty-Five, envisioning a "new New England cuisine," with the kind of seasonal farm-to-table cooking they'd loved in California. With Chef Corry in the kitchen and Michelle at the front of the house (and curating the 3,000 wines in their cellar), from the beginning Five Fifty-Five earned rave reviews, and in 2007 Chef Corry was named one of *Food & Wine* magazine's top ten best new chefs.

The two-level restaurant, named for its address, is in an historic firehouse that held horse-drawn fire trucks in the 1850s. Now the building is marked by a copper-hooded open kitchen, visible to diners on both the first floor and the mezzanine, which is edged in banisters made from Maine hardwoods. The menu changes regularly, with offerings that combine fine dining with playful twists: signature Lobster Mac & Cheese comes with large chunks of meat, homemade pasta, and a rich cheese sauce, while Mary Had a Little . . . Lamb pairs grilled and braised lamb with shaved goat parmesan, roasted squash, and a zesty oregano sauce. Next door, at the Point Five Lounge, opened in 2006, the bar menu includes fried olives stuffed with local blue cheese, a burger topped with house-made kimchi, and oysters by the half dozen. Committed to hospitality, the Corrys serve exquisite food without pretension—no mean feat.

For Five Fifty-Five's classic Lobster Risotto, lobster stock can be prepared a day in advance and refrigerated until needed. Perfect for dinner guests, the Grilled Octopus with Toasted Quinoa, Chorizo Butter, and Pickled Green Tomatoes takes a little advanced planning. Keep in mind that the Pickled Green Tomatoes need to absorb their brine for

at least a week before serving, and will keep for several more weeks if refrigerated. The octopus must brine overnight and roast for up to 8 hours before grilling, and the quinoa must be made with enough time to chill before serving.

Five Fifty-Five Lobster Risotto

(SERVES 6)

3 live Maine lobsters, each about 1½ pounds
3 quarts vegetable broth or court bouillon (see note 1)

1 teaspoon extra virgin olive oil
1 tablespoon unsalted butter
1 large shallot, minced
1 tablespoon minced garlic
1½ cups lobster stock (use your favorite recipe or
    see Salt Exchange's, page 152)
½ cup Arborio rice
½ cup dry white wine

2 ounces smoked squash puree (see note 2)
2 ounces mascarpone
½ cup diced, lightly roasted butternut squash
Lemon juice, to taste
Chopped chives, to taste
Salt to taste

3 ounces ricotta
2 tablespoons toasted pumpkin seeds
2–3 brussels sprouts, leaves separated and flash fried,
    for garnish

To cook the lobster: In a large pot over medium heat, bring vegetable broth or court bouillon to 160°F. Plunge lobsters, one at a time, into broth and partially cook, 5–7 minutes. Remove from water and set aside until cooled. When cool enough to handle, pick the lobster meat, keeping claws as intact as possible.

To make the risotto: In a large heavy-bottomed pot over medium-low heat, combine olive oil and butter, and add shallot and garlic, sweating them until they're fragrant but not browned. Meanwhile, in a separate pot, bring lobster stock to a boil. Add rice to the shallot and garlic mixture and stir to coat. Pour in wine, stirring until it's absorbed.

Add lobster stock to the mixture, ¼ cup at a time, stirring often. When rice is tender, stir in smoked squash puree, mascarpone, diced squash, and partially cooked lobster meat. Cook for 1–2 minutes, until lobster is fully cooked. Season to taste with lemon juice, chives, and salt.

To serve: Ladle risotto into shallow bowls, reserving lobster claws. Add a dollop of ricotta to each bowl. Garnish with poached claws, crispy brussels sprouts, and roasted pumpkin seeds.

Note 1: To make court bouillon, coarsely chop 1 leek, 1 carrot, and 1 rib of celery. In a large pot, combine 3 quarts water with chopped vegetables, 5 cloves of peeled and mashed garlic, 2 cups red wine vinegar, 2 sprigs fresh thyme, 3 bay leaves, 1 tablespoon white peppercorns, and 2 teaspoons sea salt. Bring mixture to a boil and cook over high heat for 15 minutes. Strain through a fine sieve. Court bouillon can be made in advance and will keep, chilled and covered, for several days in the refrigerator.

Note 2: To make smoked squash puree, peel and dice 1 butternut squash. Smoke over applewood chips for 5 minutes. Place in a nonreactive saucepan and add heavy cream, just to cover. Over medium-low heat, gently simmer until tender. Puree in a food processor until smooth, then season to taste with salt and freshly squeezed lemon juice.

Grilled Octopus with Toasted Quinoa, Chorizo Butter & Pickled Green Tomatoes

(SERVES 4)

For the pickled green tomatoes:

10 small green tomatoes, tops and bottoms scored

1 carrot, roughly chopped

1 rib celery, roughly chopped

1 onion, roughly chopped

Extra virgin olive oil

1 quart water

2 quarts white vinegar

½ cup salt

For the chorizo butter:

2 tablespoon minced chorizo

¼ cup (½ stick) unsalted butter, softened

1 tablespoon lemon juice

1 tablespoon chopped fresh chives

1 tablespoon salt

For the octopus:

1 whole octopus, cleaned weight approximately
    1 pound

3 cloves garlic, peeled

1 carrot, roughly chopped

1 onion, roughly chopped

1 rib celery, roughly chopped

1 tablespoon black peppercorns

1 bunch fresh thyme

For the quinoa:

1 cup quinoa, rinsed

¼ cup extra virgin olive oil

2 tablespoons sherry vinegar

1 red pepper, diced

1 tablespoon chopped chives

Salt, to taste

4 scallions

Extra virgin olive oil

1 cup chicken stock

To make the pickled green tomatoes: Place green tomatoes in a large glass jar or nonreactive bowl that's large enough to accommodate 3 quarts of brining liquid. In a large pot over low heat, sweat the carrot, celery, and onion in a splash of olive oil, cooking until tender. Add water and vinegar, increase heat to medium-high, and bring to a boil. Add salt and return liquid to a boil. When salt has dissolved, remove mixture from heat and pour hot liquid over tomatoes. Chill tomatoes in brine, allowing them to pickle for at least 1 week.

To make the chorizo butter: Combine all ingredients, mixing thoroughly. Place in a bowl, cover, and chill until ready to use.

Clean octopus and remove "beak."

Preheat oven to 250°F. In a deep baking pan, scatter garlic, carrot, onion, celery, peppercorns, and thyme. Rinse octopus and place in baking dish. Cover tightly with foil and roast dry for 6–8 hours, until tender. The octopus and vegetables will release enough liquid to braise the octopus. When tender, remove octopus from pan and cool.

Brush octopus with extra virgin olive oil and grill until lightly charred. Cut into large pieces and set aside. To make the quinoa, in a small saucepan over medium high heat, lightly toast rinsed quinoa in 1 tablespoon olive oil. Pour in enough water or stock to cover and simmer until al dente, 5–8 minutes. Remove from heat and cool. Toss

cooled quinoa with remaining 3 tablespoons olive oil, vinegar, red pepper, and chives. Add salt to taste.

To assemble the dish: Brush scallions with olive oil and grill, lightly charring on all sides. Remove from heat and finely chop.

In a large sauté pan over medium heat, combine octopus, chicken stock, 4 ounces chorizo butter, 4 teaspoons finely chopped pickled green tomatoes, and 4 teaspoons finely chopped grilled scallions. Bring to a simmer and reduce until octopus is glazed, approximately 3 minutes. Serve with chilled quinoa salad.

Gorgeous Gelato

434 Fore Street
(207) 699-4309
WWW.GORGEOUSGELATO.COM
Chef/Owners: Donato Giovine and Mariagrazia Zanardi

Fifteen years ago, when newlyweds Donato Giovine and Mariagrazia Zanardi visited the United States from Milan for their honeymoon, the seed of a dream was planted: Visiting cities across the country, they imagined a life in America. At the time, it was just a fantasy, but nearly a decade later, when their children were about to start school, the couple, who were ready to make a big change in life, realized that it was now or never. Giovine had his own packaging company and Zanardi taught Spanish, but both had always loved gelato, and over the course of several years, they each attended rigorous courses in the process and chemistry of the frozen treat. As Zanardi notes, "You can buy the recipes, but if you understand how the ingredients work together, you can try new things." Settling in Portland, the couple opened Gorgeous Gelato in winter of 2010—not prime gelato season. But the offerings were so delicious that they've built a loyal fan base, who brave any weather for a taste of classic Italian gelato in flavors like Stracciatella, Pistachio, Bacio, Zabaione, and Limoncello. Sorbettos are made from fresh fruits, and while many ingredients come from Maine farms, certain ingredients—Sicilian pistachios, Piedmontese hazelnuts, Lavazza coffees—are imported from Italy to ensure that flavors keep their European character.

Starting with gelato by the scoop and the pint, they've gradually added a variety of treats to their menu. Lavazza espresso drinks were an early addition, and tarts, gelato cakes, and cannoli stuffed with gelato have followed. While their gelato recipes are top

secret, Affogato and Macedonia di Gelato are delicious, elegant, and simple to make at home. Affogato, a combination of cold gelato and hot espresso, is a wonderful afternoon pick-me-up, while Macedonia di Gelato, a seasonal fruit salad with gelato on top, makes a perfect end to a summer luncheon. Scoop your favorite premium gelato into a beautiful serving dish, and savor a taste of Milan via Portland.

AFFOGATO

(SERVES 1)

2 scoops gelato
1 fresh shot of espresso
Whipped cream, lightly sweetened
Shake of cocoa
Espresso bean, for garnish

In a glass serving dish, arrange 2 scoops of your favorite gelato. These can be the same flavor or two different flavors, depending on your preference. Pour a hot, freshly made shot of espresso over the top of the gelato (it will begin to melt, so assemble the dessert quickly). Spoon or decoratively pipe whipped cream over the top, sprinkle with a shake of unsweetened cocoa, and garnish with an espresso bean, if desired. Serve immediately.

MACEDONIA DI GELATO

(SERVES 1)

2 scoops gelato or sorbetto
Fresh seasonal fruit
Whipped cream, lightly sweetened

In a glass serving dish, arrange 2 scoops of either gelato or sorbetto. These can be the same flavor or different, depending upon your preference. Decoratively arrange fresh seasonal fruits around the scoops—Mariagrazia recommends strawberries, blackberries, cherries, peaches, shaved coconut, bananas, or even lychee nuts. Top with a dollop of whipped cream and serve immediately.

GRACE

15 CHESTNUT STREET
(207) 828-4422
WWW.RESTAURANTGRACE.COM
CHEF: PETE SUELTENFUSS; OWNER: ANNE VERRILL

Down a narrow street behind City Hall, a discreet sign on a red brick wall reads "Grace." The soaring spires and stained glass of a Methodist church, built in 1859, tower above, but through the heavy doors, the prayer books have been replaced by menus (cleverly disguised as hymnals), and where the altar once stood, there is now an open kitchen, helmed by Chef Pete Sueltenfuss. Long deconsecrated, the church had been abandoned for several years before owner Anne Verrill undertook dramatic renovations to transform Grace into a restaurant and event space. Opened in the summer of 2009, the space retains its historic grandeur by keeping details alive: wires from an unsalvageable organ have been twisted into napkin rings, the windows have been painstakingly restored, and the dark wood details of the former choir loft have been polished to a deep shine. On the ground floor, pews have been replaced by tables and a circular bar that turns out heavenly cocktails. After a few of these, patrons have been known to go searching for the confessional, and a group of women dressed as nuns once broke into song on the upper balcony.

On a varied menu of what Verrill and Chef Sueltenfuss term "new American casual gourmet," offerings range from simple fried green beans and the house Grace Burger to salt-cured foie gras and a Coast of Maine Cassoulet. While the cassoulet is time-consuming to prepare, it's well worth the effort, especially for a party. If guests are restless, give them a few glasses of Grace's Heated Affair Cocktail and all will be forgiven.

Coast of Maine Cassoulet

(SERVES 4)

For the salt cod:

1 pound salt cod
2 cups milk
2 sprigs fresh thyme

For the beans:

2 cups flageolet beans soaked in salted water
    for 24 hours
1 medium onion, diced
1 fennel bulb, diced
1 head garlic, split into cloves
2 sprigs fresh rosemary
2 sprigs fresh thyme

For the seafood sausage:

1 pound fresh cod fillet, preferably tail
1 egg white
1 cup heavy cream
½ pound scallops, cleaned, with membranes removed
Meat from 2 (1-pound) lobsters, steamed and diced
Fresh lemon juice, to taste
Salt and freshly ground black pepper
2 feet natural hog casing (if unavailable,
    substitute plastic wrap)

For the clams and mussels:

1 large white onion, diced
1 fennel bulb, diced
2 heads garlic, split into cloves
4 sprigs fresh thyme
2 fresh bay leaves
2 tablespoons unsalted butter
20 littleneck clams
3 pounds mussels
2 cups dry white wine

For the bread crumbs:

2 cups panko (or your favorite bread crumbs)
½ cup rendered duck fat or unsalted butter

To prepare the salt cod: Place it in a large nonreactive container and cover with cold water. Refrigerate for 24 hours, changing the water 4–5 times. Remove the salt cod from the water and place it in a large saucepan, covering with milk and thyme sprigs. Slowly simmer over low heat until the cod flakes when tested with a fork. Remove from liquid and cool.

To cook the beans: Wrap all of the vegetables in cheesecloth, tying the top with string. Place the beans in a large heavy-bottomed saucepan with the vegetables and cover with cold water. Cook over medium heat until the beans are tender, about 1 hour. Discard the vegetables and cool the beans in their cooking liquid.

To make the seafood sausage: Place a large mixing bowl in the refrigerator to chill. In a food processor, puree the fresh cod with the egg white until very smooth. While continuing to process, slowly drizzle in the cream until it has been fully incorporated. Spoon cod mixture into the chilled mixing bowl. Dice the scallops and lobster meat and fold into the cod mixture. Season with lemon juice, salt, and pepper.

Using a sausage stuffer: Fill the hog casing with the sausage mixture, twisting into 6-inch links. If using plastic wrap, lay a large sheet on the counter. Put half of the mixture on the plastic in an even cylindrical shape, so it resembles a sausage. Being careful to not leave any air pockets, wrap the sausage in the plastic as tightly as possible and tie the ends with butcher's twine. Repeat with the remaining half of sausage mixture.

Fill a large pot with enough water to submerge the cased sausages, and bring to 170°F. Gently place the sausages in the water and cover with a kitchen towel to make sure they stay submerged.

Being careful not to let the water exceed 170°F, cook the sausages until they reach an internal temperature of 150°F. Remove from the water and immediately submerge in ice water and chill completely.

To cook the clams and mussels: Divide the vegetables and herbs into two equal portions. Place two separate saucepans over medium-low heat, melting 1 tablespoon butter in each pan. Add one portion of vegetables and herbs to each saucepan, stirring until vegetables have softened. Add the clams to one pan and the mussels to the other. Add 1 cup of wine to the mussels and 1 cup to the clams, cover, and steam until the shellfish are just open. The mussels will take much less time than the clams. Strain the liquid and reserve. Cool the shellfish and pick the meat from the shells, discarding the empty shells and any that did not open during the cooking process.

To make the bread crumbs: Heat the duck fat or butter in a sauté pan over medium-high heat until fat is fully melted. Add the bread crumbs and sauté until lightly golden, shaking the pan to toast evenly. Season with salt and pepper and drain onto paper towels.

To assemble the dish: Preheat oven to 425°F. Strain off most of the bean liquid and discard. Warm the beans in a large saucepan over medium heat. Add the reserved liquid from the shellfish and simmer until most of the liquid has been absorbed by the beans, about 15 minutes. Break the salt cod into pieces and add it and the shellfish to the beans. Cook until all of the ingredients are warm, then pour into a large casserole dish. Cut the sausage into pieces and scatter on top of the beans. Cover with an even layer of bread crumbs and bake until the sausage is heated through and the bread crumbs are deep golden brown. Serve hot.

Perfect Pairing

HEATED AFFAIR COCKTAIL

(SERVES 1)

2 ounces infused tequila (recipe to the right)
¾ ounce Cointreau
¾ ounce fresh orange juice
1 ounce fresh lemon juice
1 ounce fresh lime juice

For each Heated Affair: Fill cocktail shaker halfway with ice. Add infused tequila, Cointreau, and fruit juices. Shake to combine. Strain into a margarita glass and garnish with candied jalapeño, a slice of lime, a strawberry wedge, or whatever else feels festive and fun.

INFUSED TEQUILA

(MAKES 1.75 LITERS INFUSED TEQUILA)

1 pineapple, trimmed
1 quart fresh strawberries, cleaned and hulled
10 fresh jalapeños
1 large bottle (1.75 liters) José Cuervo
   Gold Tequila

To make the infused tequila: Thinly slice pineapple, strawberries, and jalapeños and place in a large nonreactive jar or container. Pour in the tequila and let steep, covered, for 3 days. When ready, strain out fruit and rebottle.

Beetroot Cupcakes with Lemon Curd & Mascarpone Frosting

(MAKES 2 DOZEN CUPCAKES)

For the lemon curd:

1 cup freshly squeezed lemon juice (approximately
    4–5 lemons)
8 egg yolks
2 whole eggs
1 cup plus 2 tablespoons sugar
1½ teaspoons unflavored powdered gelatin
    (½ envelope)
1 cup (2 sticks) unsalted butter, softened

For the beetroot cupcake:

½ cup plus 1 tablespoon sugar
½ cup brown sugar
3 cups all-purpose flour
1 teaspoon baking powder
½ teaspoon baking soda
½ teaspoon ground ginger
½ teaspoon ground cinnamon
Pinch of salt
2 eggs, at room temperature
6 tablespoons skim milk
6 tablespoons canola oil
2 medium beets, grated

For the mascarpone frosting:

2 cups mascarpone (approximately 1 pound)
1 vanilla bean
1 cup sifted confectioners' sugar
1 teaspoon orange flower water

Grated radish for garnish (optional)

To make the lemon curd: In a medium-size heavy-bottomed saucepan whisk together lemon juice, egg yolks, whole eggs, and sugar. Over low heat, warm mixture until it comes to a simmer, and cook, stirring continuously, for 5 minutes. While lemon mixture is heating, soften gelatin in 2 tablespoons cold water. Remove lemon mixture from heat and add softened gelatin, whisking to incorporate. Add butter to the curd, whisking vigorously or mixing it with a stick blender. Pass the curd through a fine mesh strainer and let cool in a mixing bowl until room temperature. Cover with plastic wrap and chill in the refrigerator for at least 3 hours before using.

To make the cupcakes: Preheat oven to 350°F. Line two 12-cup muffin tins with paper cupcake liners. In a large bowl, whisk together sugars, flour, baking powder, baking soda, ginger, cinnamon, and salt. In a smaller bowl, lightly beat eggs with milk and oil. Add to dry ingredients, stirring until just blended, then add the grated beets and fold to combine. Spoon batter into prepared muffin tins, filling each cup approximately two-thirds full. Bake for 10 minutes, or until a toothpick comes out clean. Cool to room temperature on a wire rack.

To make the frosting: Beat the mascarpone until soft using an electric mixer on medium speed. Scrape the seeds from the vanilla bean into the softened cheese, and add the sifted confectioners' sugar and orange flower water. Mix for 1 minute to incorporate.

To assemble the cupcakes: Preheat oven to 325°F. Cut off the tops of the cupcakes and place them on a cookie sheet. Toast in the oven until dry, approximately 10 minutes, then crumble and place in a small bowl. Using a pastry bag and tip, fill the center of each cupcake with 2 teaspoons of chilled lemon curd. Ice tops with mascarpone frosting, sprinkling toasted cupcake crumbs around the sides. If desired, garnish with grated radish for an extra fresh flavor.

Green Elephant Vegetarian Bistro

608 Congress Street
(207) 347-3111
WWW.GREENELEPHANTMAINE.COM
Chef/Owner: Danai "Dan" Sriprasert
Co-Owner: Nattask "Bob" Wongsaichua

Growing up in Thailand, Chef Danai Sriprasert spent many mornings beside his mother, who owned a restaurant, prepping ingredients for her kitchen: peeling garlic, chopping onions, making curry paste. Learning to cook at her side, Chef Sriprasert began developing his own style, a mix of Asian influences that range from traditional Thai food to Indian curries and Chinese stir-fries. Since opening Green Elephant Vegetarian Bistro in October of 2007, Chef Sriprasert has made Asian-inspired vegetarian and vegan food the focus of his menu. In a fun space, decorated with oversized forks and spoons and named for Thailand's traditional symbol of luck and prosperity, the elephant, the offerings run the gamut from the popular Tofu Tikka Masala to the addictively rich vegan Chocolate Orange Mousse Pie. Located in the downtown Arts District near the Maine College of Art and the Portland Museum of Art, the restaurant numbers among its patrons hip young art students, families plying toddlers with crunchy house-made Soy Nuggets, and professionals gathered for lunch meetings. According to the staff, many seem embarrassed to admit that they're carnivores, and are amazed by their satisfaction at the end of the meal.

With ingredients sourced as locally as possible, staples on the menu include Maine-made Heiwa Tofu (www.heiwatofu.com) and Lalibela Farms Tempeh (www.lalibelafarm .com). With a touch of Maine maple syrup, the Fried Brussels Sprouts and Wild Mushrooms balance earthy umami with a hint of sweetness, while the Chocolate Orange Mousse Pie is enough to make even the most committed omnivore think vegan.

FRIED BRUSSELS SPROUTS & WILD MUSHROOMS
(SERVES 4)

Canola oil for deep frying
1 pound brussels sprouts, washed, trimmed,
   and cut in half
1 tablespoon extra virgin olive oil
¾ cup wild mushrooms (such as black
   trumpets, cremini), sliced
1 tablespoon tamari soy sauce
1½ teaspoons Maine maple syrup
Sea salt, to taste
Pinch of freshly ground black pepper

In a medium-size pot, pour canola oil to a depth of 3 inches. Heat the oil to 350°F. Deep fry the brussels sprouts, stirring occasionally, until very dark brown and almost charred but not burnt, about 3 minutes. Remove the brussels sprouts with a skimmer and place in a large bowl.

In a large, heavy-bottomed skillet over high heat, heat the olive oil. Add mushrooms and sauté until they are brown and just tender, about 5 minutes. Add fried brussels sprouts and stir to mix. Pour in tamari and maple syrup, then add sea salt and pepper to taste. Stir well, adjust seasonings, and transfer mixture to a serving platter. Serve warm.

CHOCOLATE ORANGE
MOUSSE PIE

(MAKES ONE 9-INCH PIE)

1 (12-ounce) package silken tofu
½ cup coconut milk
2 tablespoons orange liqueur (optional)
12 ounces semisweet vegan chocolate chips
1 (9-inch) prepared chocolate graham
    cracker crust
Sliced, toasted almonds and grated
    orange peel for garnish

Blend tofu, coconut milk, and orange
liqueur in a food processor until just
smooth.

In a double boiler, melt chocolate chips.
Cool slightly, then pour into food processor
and blend with tofu mixture until creamy.
Pour mixture into chocolate graham
cracker crust. Chill in refrigerator for at least
2 hours. Garnish with toasted almonds and
orange peel before serving.

THE PORTLAND FARMERS' MARKET

Founded in 1768, the Portland Farmers' Market has the distinction of being one of the oldest continuously operating farmers' markets in the country. Originally housed in the lower floor of the Town Hall, the market began as a central location for the peddlers who went door-to-door selling lobsters, mollusks, and fresh vegetables from makeshift carts. First created to serve the 136 families that lived on the peninsula, it was in its early years by ordinance Portland's exclusive source of fresh meat. In 1805, the market moved to Monument Square (then called Hay Market Square), and though the next century and a half brought several more moves, the Farmers' Market returned to Monument Square in 1990, where it's stayed ever since, expanding on summer Saturdays to include a morning market in Deering Oaks Park. Today the market is going strong, serving the entire Portland area, with nearly fifty farmers and artisans coming weekly to sell everything from pasture-raised pork to lacto-fermented vegetables, homemade face creams to handcrafted birdhouses.

HAVANA SOUTH

WWW.HAVANAMAINE.COM
CHEF/OWNER: CASSADY PAPPAS
CO-OWNER: MICHAEL BOLAND

Until its closing in early 2012, this outpost of Bar Harbor's popular restaurant Havana, which received national attention when President Obama and the First Lady dined there on a vacation date night, brought a Latin flavor to the Old Port. Stretching along the cobbled pedestrian walkway of Wharf Street, the restaurant had a warm and lively atmosphere; Wednesday nights brought live Cuban music, with the packed bar spontaneously erupting into impromptu dance. With open outdoor seating, arched brick entryways, and vivid orange walls, the space felt a hemisphere away from New England.

In the kitchen, Chef Cassady Pappas adapted his Bar Harbor menu of seasonal American dishes with a Latin flair for the Old Port crowd. At Havana, classic seafood paella, Peruvian chicken, and churrasco (hanger steak with chimichurri sauce) sit

beside gnocchi finished with pepitas, Maine crab cakes with jalapeño orange aioli, and shortrib empanadas with poblano peppers and turnips. A Maine native, Chef Pappas began his career at age thirteen in his uncle's seafood restaurant in Bucksport, but after a four-year tour in the Marine Corps, he decided to expand his repertoire and eventually became the executive chef and co- owner of several acclaimed restaurants Down East. His signature paella incorporates the best of Maine's seafood along with spicy chorizo and fragrant saffron. Surprisingly quick to assemble, the recipe can be doubled for a party; simply allow more time for the rice to cook.

Havana South's Maine Paella

(SERVES 4)

1 tablespoon extra virgin olive oil

2 chicken thighs

2 links dried chorizo, thinly sliced

1 Spanish onion, diced

2 cloves garlic, minced

2 cups Arborio rice

1 quart chicken stock

Pinch of saffron

8 large scallops, cleaned and membranes removed

1 whole lobster, cooked and picked

¼ pound mussels, cleaned, with beards removed

6 ounces Maine shrimp

3 ounces peas

Chopped fresh parsley, for garnish

Preheat oven to 350°F. In a large heavy-bottomed pan over high heat, heat olive oil until it shimmers. Add the chicken thighs and sear on both sides, 2–3 minutes per side. Remove from heat and place in the oven to finish, about 10 minutes. When chicken is cooked through and juices run clear when pierced with a fork, remove pan from oven. Allow chicken to cool to room temperature, then shred meat and reserve.

In a large pot over medium heat, cook the sliced chorizo for 2–3 minutes, until the fat is rendered out. Add the onion and garlic, sautéing until the onion is translucent. Add the rice, stirring to coat. Reduce heat to medium-low.

In a saucepan, warm chicken stock over medium-high heat, and stir in saffron. Pour enough stock into the rice to cover. Stir occasionally to prevent sticking, and when stock is absorbed, stir in the rest of the liquid. Cook for 2 minutes, then add the scallops. Stir in the lobster claw meat, cooking for 1 minute more. Add mussels, and let cook until liquid is almost completely absorbed. Add lobster tail meat, shrimp, and peas. Turn the heat to high for 1 minute to form a crust on the bottom of the pot, then garnish with chopped fresh parsley and serve.

Hot Suppa!

703 Congress Street
(207) 871-5005
www.hotsuppa.com
Chef/Owners: Moses and Alec Sabina

In 2004, brothers Moses and Alec Sabina embarked on a life-changing journey. Portland natives, the two loved Southern food, to which Moses had been introduced while at college in Sewanee, Tennessee, and "neighborhood joints," places free of pretension, where regulars come in to find their coffee already poured. The brothers went on an eating tour of the South, seeking out diners, fish fries, barbecue pits, and out-of-the-way soul food stops. Upon their return to Portland, they began to look for a space of their own, and in 2006 Hot Suppa! opened in an old Victorian in the West End.

Moses, an alum of Cornell University's Hotel School, mans the kitchen, turning out thick sandwiches, barbecue, and breakfast hash so renowned that it's earned mention in *Bon Appétit* magazine. The easygoing vibe and daily breakfast service attract a

cross-section of Portland, from young hipsters in search of restorative Bloody Marys to professionals holding morning meetings to regulars like Hollis McLaughlin, a thirty-year veteran of the city's breakfast restaurants—described by Chef Sabina as "the fastest and friendliest busser Portland's ever known"—for whom "The Hollis," the basic Hot Suppa! breakfast of two eggs, hash browns, bacon, and toast, is named.

To keep the menu fresh, Chef Sabina makes at least one trip south each year, but there are some dishes so popular that they never change, including the Fried Green Tomatoes. At Hot Suppa! they're served in a variety of ways: on their own with a side of remoulade sauce, in fried green eggs Benedict, replacing ripe tomatoes in a fried green BLT (pictured on page 105), and with smoked Maine bay scallops. FGTs, as they're called at Hot Suppa!, are seasoned with a spice mix that Chef Sabina makes in quantity and keeps around in an airtight container for any dish that might need "an extra kick." Be careful when mixing, he warns, as the concoction has been known to induce sneezing fits!

FRIED GREEN TOMATOES

(SERVES 6)

For the FGT seasoning:

5 tablespoons garlic powder
2 tablespoons cayenne pepper
1 tablespoon paprika
1 teaspoon black pepper

For the fried green tomatoes:

1 cup all-purpose flour
3 tablespoons FGT seasoning, divided
2 eggs
1 cup buttermilk
2 cups panko bread crumbs
2 green tomatoes

Vegetable oil for frying
Salt and black pepper, to taste

To make the FGT seasoning: Combine all ingredients in a small bowl. Store in an airtight container for future use.

To make the fried green tomatoes: Set up three bowls for breading: one for flour, one for eggs and buttermilk, and one for panko bread crumbs. In the first bowl, combine flour with 1 tablespoon of FGT seasoning, whisking to combine. Crack eggs into the second bowl and beat well. Add buttermilk and 1 tablespoon of FGT seasoning and whisk together. In the third bowl, combine panko with the remaining 1 tablespoon of FGT seasoning.

Slice off the tops and bottoms of the tomatoes. Slice tomatoes into ¼-inch-thick slices. Working in batches, dredge three to four slices of tomato lightly with flour. Tap off the excess flour and dip slices into the egg-buttermilk mixture. Coat well and let excess drip off each slice before coating with seasoned panko crumbs. While they're in

the bowl, gently pat both sides of each tomato slice to ensure an even coating of crumbs.

Pour 1 inch of vegetable oil into a deep cast iron skillet or Dutch oven and, over high heat, bring oil to 360°F. Working in batches, fry three to four tomato slices at a time, flipping once and cooking until each side is evenly golden brown. Remove from oil and place on paper towels to drain. Season immediately with salt and pepper. Allow excess oil to continue draining onto the paper towels while tomato cools slightly. Serve hot.

HUGO'S

88 MIDDLE STREET
(207) 774-8538
WWW.HUGOS.NET
CHEF/OWNER: ANDREW TAYLOR
CO-OWNERS: ARLIN SMITH AND MIKE WILEY

New England native Chef Rob Evans began his career as an electrician, but after quickly becoming bored with wiring, his "love of eating turned into a love of cooking." A self-taught chef, he's now been cooking professionally for more than two decades, and his culinary skills have been sharpened in kitchens from Virginia's acclaimed Inn at Little Washington to Thomas Keller's renowned French Laundry in Napa Valley, California.

Returning to Maine in 2000, Chef Evans and his wife and partner Nancy Pugh bought an established restaurant at the edge of the Old Port, Hugo's Portland Bistro, which had been named after the previous owner's son. Though Chef Evans's culinary style was radically different, the couple made minimal changes to the décor, and decided to simply shorten the name. In the years that have followed, Hugo's has become synonymous with a progressive New England cuisine: the carefully crafted dishes come beautifully plated, with complex flavors created from unexpected ingredients.

The tasting menus, in particular, have brought Hugo's national acclaim, and earned Chef Evans nominations for the Best Chef in the Northeast award by the James Beard Foundation in 2007 and 2008, and a win in 2009. Chef Evans has also appeared nationally on television, and in 2011 he was the winning contestant on the Food Network's popular show *Chopped*. In daily life, however, Chef Evans is more likely found sharpening his knives than resting on his laurels and, eager for new culinary adventures, in 2012, he sold the restaurant to several members of his staff, current Chef/Owner Andrew Taylor, General Manager Arlin Smith, and cook Mike Wiley. The three plan to continue in Hugo's beloved style, with one exciting addition: an adjacent oyster bar called Eventide Oyster Company.

It goes without saying that the menu at Hugo's changes regularly to include what's seasonally available, be it locally foraged

mushrooms, seafood that can be harvested for a few brief weeks, or house-made charcuterie from a custom-slaughtered pig.

Lomo, a Spanish air-cured pork loin, is traditionally served shaved, and it appears on charcuterie plates, or as tapas with accompaniments such as olives, grapes, melon, and cheese. It can also be piled on sandwiches, or served as it is at Hugo's, with mixed seasonal greens, a quick vegetable pickle, and aerated mustard. When making Chef Evans's Air Cured Lomo, look for the best pasture-raised pork you can find, and keep in mind that you'll need to start at least two and a half months before you plan to serve the charcuterie (for a Superbowl party, you'll begin curing the meat before Thanksgiving). Insta Cure No. 2, a sodium nitrate cure specifically designed for air-cured meats, can be ordered online from www.sausagemaker.com. As with all charcuterie, use an accurate scale to ensure proper proportions for the cure. A staple in the molecular gastronomer's pantry, xanthan gum can be found in most natural food markets. Soda guns can be found online, or at better kitchen stores.

TAKING FARM-TO-TABLE A FEW STEPS FURTHER

As the farm-to-table restaurant movement gains momentum around the country, Maine's chefs are taking things a step further. Longtime proponents of local ingredients—Portland's acclaimed chef Sam Hayward, James Beard's 2004 Best Chef in the Northeast, has been naming the provenance of meats and vegetables on his menu for decades—many chefs are now beginning to grow their own.

On small farms that ring Portland's metro area, chefs like Masa Miyake, proprietor of Miyake and Pai Men Miyake, and Lee Skawinski of Cinque Terre (page 48) and Vignola (page 174) are growing offbeat vegetables, fresh herbs, and some of the meat served at their restaurants. Others, like Rob Evans originally of Hugo's and now of Duckfat (page 55), go "whole hog," buying entire animals that they butcher and cure themselves. At the annual Twenty Mile Meal, a fundraiser for local nonprofit Cultivating Community, dozens of chefs work exclusively with ingredients grown or gathered within twenty miles of Portland, making dishes that can range from kelp slaw to pulled pork on goat cheese polenta to ground-cherry cupcakes. With creativity and passion, many of Portland's best chefs work within the state's short northern growing season, embracing Maine's agricultural heritage and bringing its unique flavors to the table.

Air-Cured Lomo with Quick Vegetable Pickle & Aerated Mustard

(SERVES A CROWD)

For the air-cured lomo:

1 pork loin, about 5 pounds
4½ ounces kosher salt
¾ ounce granulated sugar
½ ounce Insta Cure No. 2
¼ ounce ground coriander
½ ounce crushed red pepper
2 ounces smoked paprika

For the quick vegetable pickle:

¼ cup granulated sugar
½ cup rice wine vinegar
2 cups water
Seasonal vegetables of choice, cleaned and
      cut into uniform pieces

For the aerated mustard:

½ cup prepared Dijon mustard
2 cups water
½ teaspoon xanthan gum

Mixed seasonal greens, for serving

To prepare the lomo: Trim the pork loin, leaving a thick layer of fat. In a medium size bowl, combine salt, sugar, Insta Cure, and spices, and rub thoroughly over the outside of the pork. Put the loin in a plastic container, seal tightly, and place in the refrigerator. Let sit for 1 week, then turn over and let sit for 1 week more.

Rinse off the salt and spice mixture with cool water. Pat pork dry with paper towels. Tie the loin with butcher's twine, creating a loop at one end. If you have the space in your refrigerator, hang the lomo to air cure for two months, or until the meat is the desired firmness. If you don't have the space to hang the meat while it cures, place it on a rack in a shallow dish in the refrigerator for two months, turning regularly so that it cures evenly.

To make the quick vegetable pickle: In a medium size saucepan over medium high heat, combine sugar, vinegar, and water and bring to a boil. Arrange vegetables in a large canning jar or nonreactive bowl. Pour boiling liquid over vegetables and let sit, covered, overnight in the refrigerator. Refrigerated, the pickle will last up to two weeks.

To make the aerated mustard: Combine all ingredients in a blender and puree. Pour the mixture into a soda gun with one charge and chill the filled gun in an ice bath for 1 hour before use.

To serve: Arrange greens on a plate and top with pickle and thin slices of lomo. Dress with aerated mustard before serving.

LOCAL 188

685 CONGRESS STREET
(207) 761-7909
WWW.LOCAL188.COM
CHEF DE CUISINE/OWNER: JAY VILLANI
EXECUTIVE CHEF: NICHOLAS NAPPI

As a young artist in the mid-1980s, Chef Jay Villani bounced in and out of kitchens in New York City while pursuing his artistic career, playing in bands, and occasionally taking off to travel the country. Always coming back to the kitchen, he started as a dishwasher, working his way up, filling in for an absentee salad guy here, a prep cook there, at stints that lasted six months to a year, until he'd absorbed the dynamics of a restaurant kitchen. "I had a resume that read like a dictionary," he says now. "Little did I know that stability and longevity were key. I blame youth."

With his wife Allison, also an artist, Villani moved to Portland in 1994, and after originally opening a tiny art gallery called the Pleasant Street Collective, the two realized that a large space combining food, wine, and art would be, as Chef Villani puts it, "more economically viable." Partnering with local artist Patrick Corrigan and high school friend

Matt Purington and his wife Kitty, they opened Local 188 in 1999, serving tapas, paella, and potent sangria in a high-ceilinged space at 188 Congress, on Longfellow Square, with an open kitchen, cheerful wall murals, and an ever changing gallery of art on the exposed brick walls.

Over the years, the restaurant has expanded, moving across the street to a larger space with two bars—one serving spirits and one overlooking the bustling kitchen—a lounge area scattered with deep velvet couches, and more table seating. The menu, still influenced by Mediterranean and "Old World Latin" flavors, has broadened to include nods to North African and Middle Eastern cuisine, though paella remains the specialty of the house.

Committed to sourcing ingredients locally, Chef Villani is actively looking for a farm on which to grow and raise vegetables and meats. In the meantime he works with local farmers, and is fostering the talents and obscure interests of his staff. Local 188 charcuterist Josh Craigue expressed interest in learning to cure meats, and now makes the house bacon and sausage, smoking them in the alley behind the restaurant. His bacon can be wood-smoked or left fresh (unsmoked); delicious either way, he swears that "if you do own a smoker, smoking will elevate your simple belly far past any store-bought bacon." When preparing the bacon, look for the optional Insta Cure No. 1, a basic charcuterie cure combining salt and sodium nitrate, at www.sausagemaker.com. To ensure proper proportions, use a calculator and an accurate metric scale to weigh the ingredients for the cure.

House-Cured Bacon, Fresh or Smoked

(MAKES ANY AMOUNT)

For every pound of skin-on pork belly, use:

10.7 grams kosher salt

2.5 grams Insta Cure No. 1 (optional, but recommended)

10.7 grams brown sugar

8.5 grams cracked black pepper

4.3 grams crushed red pepper flake

1 liquid ounce maple syrup

Trim the pork belly to a rectangle of even thickness, to ensure an even cure. Weigh the trimmed pork and calculate the amount needed for each of the curing ingredients. Mix the salt, Insta Cure, sugar, spices, and maple syrup until the cure is thoroughly combined. Spread half the cure in the bottom of a nonreactive pan that is just big enough to hold the whole belly. Place the pork on top of the mixture, then spread the other half of the cure over the belly, making sure to coat evenly. Cover tightly with plastic wrap.

Refrigerate pork belly for 1 week, flipping the meat over every day. At the end of the week, unwrap the belly and rinse off any excess cure with cool water. If you are planning not to smoke the bacon, simply remove the skin and cook directly. If you do plan to smoke the meat, leave the skin on and smoke the belly at 160°F for 6–8 hours, until an internal temperature of 160°F is reached. Remove the skin, slice as thickly as desired, and cook.

LOCAL EGG BAKED IN DELICATA SQUASH

(SERVES 8)

2 delicata squash

2 Italian eggplants

6 red peppers, roasted (see note)

2 tablespoons sherry vinegar

1 tablespoon chopped shallots

2 tablespoons chopped fresh oregano

1 tablespoon unsalted butter, chilled

Salt to taste

1 cup grapeseed oil

2½ tablespoons ground fenugreek seed

1 tablespoon ground coriander

1 tablespoon turmeric

1 tablespoon whole black pepper

3 teaspoons ground ginger

1 vanilla pod, split

3 star anise

Canola oil, for pan

8 eggs, preferably farm fresh

Preheat oven to 375°F. Slice delicata squash into rings approximately 1½ inches thick. Arrange on a baking dish and bake until tender, about 30 minutes. Remove from oven and let cool to room temperature. Reduce oven temperature to 350°F.

While squash is baking, cut eggplants into cubes, sprinkle with salt, and place in a colander to drain. When drained, scatter eggplant cubes on a roasting pan and cover tightly with aluminum foil. Bake in a 350°F oven for 20 minutes, or until tender.

Place baked eggplant, roasted red peppers, sherry vinegar, shallots, and oregano in a blender and puree until smooth. Pass mixture through a chinois or fine strainer into a small saucepan and whisk in chilled butter. Adjust salt to taste, and keep sauce warm until ready to serve.

In a separate small saucepan over low heat, warm 1 cup grapeseed oil and add fenugreek, coriander, turmeric, black pepper, ginger, split vanilla pod, and star anise. Remove from heat and let spices infuse the oil as the mixture cools to room temperature. Strain cooled curry oil through a coffee filter into a jar or small bowl.

Preheat oven to 450°F. Heat an ovenproof sauté pan filmed with canola oil over medium heat, and arrange baked delicata squash rings in the pan. Crack an egg into the middle of each ring and place pan in the oven for 10 minutes, or until the egg whites are set. To serve, spoon eggplant-pepper sauce onto each plate, top with a squash ring with a baked egg in the center, and drizzle with curry oil.

Note: To roast red peppers: Simply char whole peppers over an open gas flame or under the broiler until skin is blackened. Place in a bowl, cover tightly with plastic wrap, and allow to steam for 10 minutes. When cool enough to handle, peel off the skin and remove stems and seeds.

LOCAL SPROUTS CAFE

649 CONGRESS STREET
(207) 899-3529
WWW.LOCALSPROUTSCOOPERATIVE.COM

With a mission to "provide people in Maine with creative local and organic food and holistic learning through cooking food for our community," the Local Sprouts Cooperative is a restaurant like no other in Portland. Incorporated as a worker-owned cooperative in 2008, the cafe moved into its current space, a former University of Southern Maine dorm cafeteria, in 2010, with nearly 200 volunteers pitching in to help with renovations. Now the cafe is furnished with tables made from reclaimed wood, the walls are adorned with murals, and the entrance features a large cob booth in the shape of a crow, made by volunteers out of earth, sand, and straw. Local bands jam regularly on a small stage, and after hours, the cafe is often host to various community events and meetings.

Rather than a single chef, the cafe and its catering operation are the work of many, with Kitchen Coordinator Meara Smith facilitating the kitchen and creation of menus. As worker-owner and co-founder, Jonah Fertig notes, the chefs have worked in various professions, both culinary and otherwise, and their backgrounds incorporate a wide range of experiences, from teaching to social work, community organizing to activism, and work in professional kitchens from fine restaurants to food pantries. The menu reflects this diversity, and while the focus is on comfort foods and on vegetarian, vegan, and gluten-free meals, house specials run the gamut, including Stone's Jerk Chicken, vegan Sprouts Bowl with vegetables, rice, beans, and Maine-made tofu or tempeh, the immensely popular Roasted Butternut Squash and Cheddar Sandwich and BLTs with locally cured bacon, served on bread baked by Bomb Diggity Bakery, a baking and creative arts program for adults with intellectual disabilities that's run from the cafe.

Local Sprouts' strong commitment to using seasonal ingredients has its challenges—notably, a short growing season that leaves winter and early spring without much in the fields. The two recipes below showcase the creativity with which the cooperative approaches the abundant squash of fall, which keep well and often last into the next year. The Roasted Butternut Squash and Cheddar Sandwich is a favorite at the cafe, and can be served either hot or cold. For the Butternut Squash Ravioli, developed by cooperative member Barry Manson, use your favorite pasta dough, or try East Ender's recipe (page 62).

Roasted Butternut Squash & Cheddar Sandwich

(MAKES 8 SANDWICHES)

For the aioli:

1 egg
1 garlic clove, minced
1 cup oil (canola, safflower, olive oil, or a mix)
Juice of ½ lemon
Salt and freshly ground black pepper, to taste

For the cranberry sauce:

2 cups cranberries
Water to cover
Local honey, to taste

1 medium butternut squash (look for one with
   a 6-inch diameter neck)
Oil to grease baking pan
Salt and freshly ground black pepper, to taste

16 thick slices of peasant or whole grain bread
½ red onion, thinly sliced
8 slices cheddar cheese
2 generous handfuls of local organic greens

To make the aioli: In a blender or the bowl of an electric mixer, beat the egg with the garlic until the mixture is frothy and slightly thickened. Slowly add the oil, drip by drip, until the mixture begins to emulsify and thicken noticeably. When you've added all the oil, pour in the lemon juice, a little at a time so the sauce doesn't get too watered down. Add salt and pepper to taste, and chill until ready to use.

To make the cranberry sauce: Place the cranberries in a small saucepan with enough water so that the berries just float. Place over high heat until the water comes to a boil, then reduce heat to a simmer. Add enough honey to lightly sweeten (start with 1/4 cup and add more if desired). Cook sauce until it begins to thicken, then remove pan from heat and cool until ready to use. Cranberry sauce will last several days in the refrigerator or can be frozen for later use.

To prepare the butternut squash: Preheat oven to 375°F. Peel squash and cut top part (above seeded hollow) into 1/4-inch squash "steaks." Save the bottom for soup or other recipes. You should have 8 steaks.

Toss the squash with a small amount of oil and salt and pepper to taste. Place on a sheet pan and roast in the oven for approximately 20 minutes, or until squash is tender.

To assemble the sandwiches: If serving hot, place slices of cheddar cheese on hot squash steaks to melt. Toast slices of bread, or brush lightly with olive oil and grill. Spread aioli and cranberry sauce on the bread slices, top with hot squash steaks and cheese, sliced red onion, greens, and a second slice of bread. If serving cold, allow the squash to cool completely before assembling.

Butternut Squash Ravioli with Sage Brown Butter

(SERVES 4–6)

9 tablespoons butter

3 tablespoons minced shallots

1 cup roasted butternut squash puree

Salt and freshly ground white pepper, to taste

3 tablespoons heavy cream

2 ounces plus 3 tablespoons grated Parmigiano Reggiano cheese

Pinch of nutmeg

1 recipe pasta dough, rolled out into wide ribbons about 1/8-inch thick

12 fresh sage leaves

1 tablespoon finely chopped fresh parsley leaves, for garnish

In a large sauté pan, over medium heat, melt 1 tablespoon of the butter. Add the shallots and sauté for 1 minute. Add the squash puree and cook until the mixture is slightly dry, about 2–3 minutes. Season with salt and white pepper. Stir in the cream and continue to cook for 2 minutes. Remove from the heat and stir in 3 tablespoons of the cheese and nutmeg to taste. Adjust seasonings to taste. Cool completely.

Cut the pasta ribbons into 3-inch squares. You will have approximately 40 pieces of dough. Place 2 teaspoons of the filling in the center of each pasta square. Bring one corner of the square to the opposite corner, forming a triangle, and pinch the two open sides to seal the filled pasta completely.

Bring a large pot of salted water to a boil. Add the pasta and cook until al dente, about 2–3 minutes or until the pasta floats and is pale in color.

Remove the pasta from the water and drain well.

Season with salt and pepper.

In a large sauté pan, melt the remaining 8 tablespoons of butter. Add the sage to the butter and continue to cook until the butter starts to brown. Remove from heat.

To serve: Divide the ravioli between the serving plates. Spoon the brown butter over the pasta. Sprinkle the remaining 2 ounces of grated cheese over the plates and garnish with parsley.

Maple's Organic

14 Gary Maietta Parkway, South Portland
(207) 899-3342
WWW.MAPLESORGANIC.COM
Owner: Kristie Green

With a serious sweet tooth and a commitment to supporting local organic producers, it was natural that when Kristie Green thought about expanding her kitchen skills to a larger scale, she would want to make a product that involved dessert and was made with ingredients that could be sourced year-round in Maine's northern climate. The granddaughter of Jack Angelone, who opened Portland's first pizza shop after the Second World War, Green grew up watching her father and aunts manage the family pizzerias and, like her grandfather, wanted to create a legacy that honored her values and could be passed to her family. Distressed by the trend toward mix-based ice creams, even among small-batch producers, Green began making gelato, starting from scratch on the stovetop with MOFGA-certified MOO milk (Maine's Own Organic, a dairy cooperative) and eggs from Sparrow Farm in Gardiner, and sourcing as much as possible—from syrup to sea salt—from Maine producers. (The "beautiful, flaky sea salt" that Green prefers comes from a company in Down East Maine that uses a solar evaporator.)

Originally available only by the scoop, Maple's Organic gelato and sorbetto are now available by the pint throughout New England, though the shift required some rebranding. The business was named for Green's border collie, Maple, whose face appeared on

the early packaging, but a new label was designed after confusion about whether the gelato was intended for dogs. Flavors include Italian classics, but devoted followers go for more exotic offerings: Cardamom-Ginger, Turkish Fig–Orange, and Sweet Tea Sorbetto. But the house favorite is Sea Salt Caramel–Almond. Says Green, "I don't think I'm actually capable of making anything tastier."

Now the mother of two, Green is proud to continue her family's business tradition. She's even begun making pizza in her retail shop, across Casco Bay in South Portland.

One of Green's favorite things about the Maine Maple Gelato is that it's made entirely from ingredients produced in the state. When making at home, be sure to use a dark, richly flavored maple syrup. You'll taste the difference.

Maine Maple Gelato

(MAKES ABOUT 1 QUART)

1 cup maple syrup, darkest available
   (Green uses a grade B dark amber)
4 egg yolks
2½ cups milk
¼ teaspoon sea salt
½ cup heavy cream

In a heatproof bowl, beat together maple syrup and egg yolks until the mixture is noticeably lightened in color. Set aside.

In a 3-quart saucepan over medium heat, bring milk and sea salt to a boil, then remove from heat. Whisking rapidly to prevent the eggs from scrambling, stream about 1 cup of the hot milk into the egg yolk mixture. Stream this mixture back into the remaining hot milk, again whisking rapidly. Add the cream, mix thoroughly, and refrigerate for several hours. When thoroughly chilled, freeze according to manufacturer's instructions in the ice cream maker of your choice.

NOSH KITCHEN BAR

551 CONGRESS STREET
(207) 553-2227
WWW.NOSHKITCHENBAR.COM
CHEF/OWNER: JASON LORING
CO-OWNERS: MATT MORAN, TOM BARR 3RD, TOBEY MOULTON

With leather couches arranged near the entrance, art depicting butcher's cuts on the walls, and daily specials like house-cured kielbasa and corned beef chalked above the long bar, Nosh is a carnivore's delight. (A T-shirt mounted on the wall advocates for the virtues of a "100% meat diet.") Serving upscale deli food—which here veers from classic Reubens to house-smoked chicken banh mi—Nosh's relaxed atmosphere and mountainous portions have kept it bustling since it opened in early 2010. The name, derived from the Yiddish term for snacking, comes from chef and co-owner Jason Loring's days at the Culinary Institute of America, where it originated as a project in his mock restaurant class. Years later, after a career that took Chef Loring from busy New York kitchens to Las Vegas's Bellagio Casino, where he worked for Todd English at the renowned Olives, the Maine native came home and teamed up with several partners to make the project a reality.

Despite its Jewish roots, the menu is far from that of a traditional kosher deli, with house favorites that include tempura bacon, "World Famous bacon dusted French fries," and the Apocalypse Now Burger, a stack of pork and beef patties topped with American cheese, bacon, foie gras, house-made mayonnaise, and cherry jam, which brought swoons from the host of the Travel Channel's hit show *Man vs. Food.* Desserts take the comfort food up a few more notches at Nosh, with s'mores, six-layer bars—like your mother used to make, but bigger—and plates of animal crackers and frosting.

Nosh batters and fries its own house-cured bacon, so when making the Tempura-Fried Bacon at home, try to use the best bacon you can find (or try out Local 188's recipe for home-cured bacon, page 112). And keep in mind that, as Chef Loring is quick to acknowledge, "It's not an everyday treat"—a little of this heavenly swine goes a long way. For the House-Brined Corned Beef, note that brining is a 30-day process, so to get ready for St. Patrick's Day, you'll need to get started in mid-February. Pink salt, a charcuterie staple, can be ordered online as Insta Cure No. 1 at www.sausagemaker.com.

TEMPURA-FRIED BACON "ELVIS STYLE"

(SERVES 6)

For the tempura batter:

1½ cups all-purpose flour, plus more for
    dredging the bacon
½ cup cornstarch
2 cups soda water

12 thick-cut strips smoked or cured bacon
Canola oil

For the peanut butter sauce:

1 quart heavy cream
1 teaspoon red chili flakes
2 cups creamy peanut butter

3 bananas
Clover honey, for serving

To make the tempura bacon: In a large bowl
combine flour and cornstarch, slowly whisking
in the soda water until the mixture is the
consistency of thick soup.

Heat canola oil in a fryer or a deep skillet until it
reaches 300°F.

Roll bacon strips in flour to cover, then drag
bacon through the batter, coating thoroughly.
Let hang for 2–3 seconds to allow excess batter
to drip off. Plunge into hot oil and remove when
crisp and golden brown. Place on paper towels to
drain excess oil.

To make the peanut butter sauce: In a 3-quart
saucepan combine heavy cream with chili flakes.
Over low heat, gently warm the mixture, whisking
in peanut butter and mixing until smooth.

To serve: Slice bananas lengthwise and place
one half on each of six plates. Lay two strips
of bacon on top and drizzle with peanut butter
sauce and honey.

HOUSE-BRINED CORNED BEEF

(SERVES 16)

30-day brine:

1 gallon water

2½ cups sugar

3½ cups kosher salt

1 teaspoon pink salt (Insta Cure No. 1)

1 teaspoon black peppercorns

1 teaspoon juniper berries

5 cloves

5 bay leaves

5 sprigs fresh thyme

2 gallons ice

8–10 pounds beef brisket, in one piece

2 cups white vinegar

2 tablespoons pickling spice

1½ teaspoons juniper berries

3 bay leaves

In a large nonreactive stock pot, combine water, sugar, kosher salt, pink salt, peppercorns, juniper berries, cloves, bay leaves, and fresh thyme, and warm over medium heat to dissolve sugar and salt. Pour into a clean plastic or nonreactive bucket (making sure to leave enough space for the meat) and add ice. Submerge the brisket and weigh it down with a plate so that it is fully covered by the brine. Refrigerate and brine for 30 days.

To cook the corned beef: Preheat oven to 275°F. Place brisket in a roasting pan or deep pot along with the vinegar, pickling spice, juniper berries, and bay leaves, and cover with water. Bring to a boil on the stove, then cover with parchment and foil and roast for 8–10 hours, until fork tender.

OLD PORT SEA GRILL

93 COMMERCIAL STREET
(207) 879-6100
WWW.THEOLDPORTSEAGRILL.COM
CHEF: DAVID CONNOLLY

On a busy stretch of Commercial Street in the heart of the historic Old Port, the Old Port Sea Grill's modern interior may seem a little anachronistic. A 250-gallon saltwater fish tank illuminates the entryway with a faint blue glow, blond wood paneling lightens the exposed brick walls, and vaguely aquatic modern art hangs above tables. The main attraction—to the eye and the palate—is a custom-poured concrete bar, seating more than fifty and curving the length of the restaurant, brimming with seafood. Piled on mounds of crushed ice, the raw bar is a thing of beauty, featuring fresh fish and shellfish, with an emphasis on the briny, cold-water oysters native to the East Coast. Here you'll find coppery Belons and rich Glidden Points from the Damariscotta River, sweet Winter Points from West Bath, and light Flying Points from Yarmouth, all with a staff eager to guide you through any unfamiliar waters.

In the dining room, the menu's focus is on seafood, with local meats and a few vegetarian entrees to round it out. A relative newcomer to Portland, Chef David Connolly relocated to Maine after years on the Chicago food scene, where he was a sous-chef at the famed Spiaggia and most recently chef de cuisine at the Wit Hotel, overseeing their two restaurants. Chef Connolly's style, which is marked by clean, bright flavors and a love of olive oil, is influenced by a childhood spent in Spain, and upon his arrival, the Old Port Sea Grill's menu was revamped and the wine list underwent a total overhaul.

The recipes below reflect his palate, and his enthusiasm for Maine's local seafood. For the Wild Maine Mussels with Fennel Cream, if you don't own a juicer, simply chop the fennel bulbs and sauté in an additional tablespoon of butter over medium-high heat for 5–7 minutes before adding cream.

Chibouste cream is a French dessert of *crème patissière* (pastry cream) beaten with whipped cream or meringue. At the Old Port Sea Grill, the Lemon Chibouste is typically served with black pepper shortbreads and macerated lemon segments. At home, garnish with lemon zest and accompany with a shortbread cookie or two.

WILD MAINE MUSSELS WITH FENNEL CREAM

(SERVES 4–8)

6 fennel heads, fronds removed, bulbs
   and stalks separated
1 quart heavy cream
1 cup Pernod
1 tablespoon coriander seed, toasted
2 star anise, toasted
2 tablespoons unsalted butter
1 shallot, sliced
2 pounds wild Maine mussels, cleaned
1 baguette, sliced

Juice the fennel bulbs, reserving all liquid.

In a 3-quart saucepan over medium-low heat, combine fennel juice, heavy cream, Pernod, and spices, and let come to a simmer. Add the fennel stalks and let the cream mixture reduce by at least one-quarter. Once reduced, strain the cream and reserve.

In a large pot over medium-high heat, melt butter, add shallots, and let sweat for 2–3 minutes. Add the mussels and the cream mixture, cover the pot, and let steam for 5–7 minutes, or until the mussels have opened. Divide between bowls and serve with baguette slices.

CASCO BAY

The sparkling waters of Casco Bay, with its wooded islands, flashing lighthouses, and abundant bird life, can seem incongruous with the cosmopolitan city at its edge. An inlet of the Gulf of Maine, the bay was originally called Aucocisco, meaning "place of herons" in the Native American language of the Abenaki. Its current name comes from the Spanish Bahía de Cascos, or Bay of Helmets, as it was christened by explorer Esteban Gómez, who mapped the coast in 1525. Portland, originally called Casco, was settled on its shores in the 1600s. The bay's many islands are collectively called the Calendar Islands because it was originally thought that there were 365 of them (revised estimates lower the number to the mid-200s), and they include residential communities, forts, lighthouses, and unpopulated rock formations. For a view of the bay, try a scenic cruise or a boat tour, which leave year-round from Portland's ferry terminal.

SEARED CASCO BAY COD
WITH HEIRLOOM CAULIFLOWER "RISOTTO" & MULLED RED WINE SAUCE

(SERVES 4)

1 head white cauliflower, roughly chopped

½ cup (1 stick) unsalted butter

Salt and pepper to taste

2 heads heirloom cauliflower, separated into florets

½ bottle dry red wine

1 cinnamon stick

2 star anise

2 tablespoons cornstarch

4 (7-ounce) fillets cod, preferably Casco Bay

2 tablespoons canola oil

Microgreens, for garnish

In a large pot over high heat, bring water to a boil, add white cauliflower, and boil for 4–5 minutes or until tender. Remove cauliflower with a slotted spoon or skimmer and allow to cool slightly. Place cooked cauliflower in a blender along with butter, salt, and pepper, and puree until smooth. Set aside.

Using the same pot, return water to a boil, add the heirloom cauliflower florets, and cook until tender, 2–3 minutes. Remove the florets and put them in an ice bath to cool quickly. Once they are cool, drain off the ice water and set the florets aside.

In a medium-size saucepan over medium-high heat, combine the red wine, cinnamon stick, and star anise and bring to a boil, reducing by half. Combine cornstarch with a small amount of warm water to make a slurry and pour into the red wine sauce, whisking to incorporate. Let cook for 1 minute, or until it begins to thicken. Allow to cool to room temperature.

To make the cod: Preheat oven to 400°F. Season cod fillets liberally on both sides with salt and pepper. Heat oil over medium-high heat in a large, heavy-bottomed, ovenproof skillet. Add cod and sear on one side for 2 minutes, then place skillet in the oven for 6 minutes or until the fish is opaque and cooked through.

While the cod is finishing in the oven, place the cauliflower puree and heirloom cauliflower florets in a small saucepan on the stovetop, and heat through.

To serve: Spoon some of the red wine sauce onto each of four plates, followed by the cauliflower cream "risotto." Place a cod fillet on top and garnish with microgreens.

LEMON CHIBOUSTE

(SERVES 6)

1 envelope unflavored gelatin
¾ cup milk
¼ cup cornstarch
¼ cup sugar
6 egg yolks
7 tablespoons freshly squeezed lemon juice

For the meringue:

¾ cup plus 1 tablespoon sugar
3½ tablespoons water
6 egg whites, at room temperature

Lemon zest, for garnish
Shortbread cookies (optional)

In a small bowl, soften gelatin in 1 tablespoon cold water. Set aside.

In a small saucepan whisk together milk and cornstarch. Heat over medium-low heat, stirring frequently, until hot. In a separate bowl, whisk together the sugar and the egg yolks until well combined. Whisking continuously, pour half of the hot milk mixture into the yolk mixture and continue whisking until the mixture comes together. Pour the yolk mixture back into the saucepan and place over medium-low heat, stirring until it thickens to a pudding-like consistency. Remove from heat, whisk in the lemon juice, and strain through a fine sieve. Mix in softened gelatin and set aside.

To make the meringue: Combine sugar and water in a small pot and set over high heat. In the bowl of an electric stand mixer, using the whisk attachment, beat the egg whites until soft peaks form. When the sugar syrup has reached 250°F, slowly pour it into the egg whites in a thin

stream, whisking on high until the mixture has cooled and is pillowy, 7–10 minutes. When the meringue is at room temperature, whisk half into the lemon custard. Using a rubber spatula, gently fold in the remaining meringue. Pipe or scoop into decorative serving dishes and chill until ready to serve. If desired, garnish with lemon zest and serve with shortbread.

WHOOPIE PIES

A deceptively simple combination of cake rounds and frosting, Whoopie Pies are so beloved by Mainers that former governor John Baldacci once celebrated them by naming a holiday in their honor. Though recipes vary, the classic pie is made of two circles of chocolate cake sandwiched around a white frosting that can be anything from vanilla buttercream to marshmallow fluff. On busy summer weekends, stands selling plastic-wrapped homemade whoopie pies line Route 1 all the way up the coast. If you're in Portland, the place to go is Cranberry Island Kitchen (52 Danforth Street; 207-774-7110). Their gourmet whoopie pies, featured on the *Martha Stewart Show* and the Food Network—where the ladies of Cranberry Island defeated Chef Bobby Flay in a "Whoopie Pie Throw-down"—are made with natural local ingredients and fillings range from classic to Cointreau. The recipes are a carefully guarded secret, but pies are available at their retail shop and, frozen, in markets across New England. For those who avoid gluten, Bam Bam Bakery (267 Commercial Street; 207-889-4100) makes a delicious, gluten-free version of the classic pie.

OTTO Pizza

576 Congress Street
(207) 773-7099
and
225 Congress Street
(207) 358-7870
www.ottoportland.com
Chef/Owners: Anthony Allen and Mike Keon

When veteran restaurateurs Anthony Allen and Mike Keon were looking for a location for OTTO Pizza, one space caught their eye: a cluttered thrift store at an intersection of Congress Street just east of the Portland Museum of Art. The location was perfect for what they envisioned—a place to get fantastic, inventive pizza by the slice—but

in the historic downtown building, it seemed unlikely that they could make the renovations necessary for a restaurant kitchen with hot pizza ovens and proper ventilation. Then, while looking more closely with a realtor, they found a working hood tucked in a dropped ceiling, installed years ago over the stove of a long defunct Peruvian restaurant. That hood, which now wafts the warm smells of garlic and cheese onto the street, sealed the deal, and in 2009 the two opened OTTO, a deliberate palindrome, with a logo that shines on the back wall like Batman's signal when headlights come up Forest Avenue.

The restaurant, with walk-up counters, shallow bars that line the walls so patrons can perch on a stool with a slice, and a décor of salvaged and vintage woodwork, has quickly expanded. Next door, at the attached wine bar Enzo, patrons can sip glasses of hearty reds and crisp whites at long tables, while their pizzas are passed through a window from the kitchen. On Munjoy Hill, OTTO's second Portland location has piano strings on the backs of its high booths (muted, so that inadvertent strumming doesn't cause cacophony), a long bar, and seasonal outdoor seating with views of the historic Eastern Cemetery across the street.

But it's the pizza that packs them in. On a classic thin crust, the creative toppings that seem initially strange have developed a cultish following. Butternut squash, herbed ricotta, and cranberries is a perennial fall favorite; spicy pulled pork and mango is addictively sweet and salty; and mashed Maine potato, bacon, and scallion (recipe on page 131) has been named one of the Best Fifty Pizzas in Fifty States by the editors of *Food Network* magazine and was featured in the Food Network television special "Pizza Outside the Box."

When making pizza, Chefs Allen and Keon recommend using a pizza stone and a wooden pizza peel (though a pizza pan or cookie sheet is fine, too). Even if you're inexperienced with a pizza stone, they encourage trying it out, since it helps produce a deliciously crunchy crust. While their dough recipe is top secret, they recommend looking online for a recipe and using their instructions for preparing the dough for toppings. A few tips are key: before you start, take off any jewelry you don't want encased in dough, let gravity do as much of the work as possible, and always work "with conviction." If you're feeling adventurous, try tossing the dough in the air as part of the stretching process!

OTTO's Basic Instructions for Pizza Preparation

(MAKES ONE 12-INCH PIZZA)

1 (8-ounce) ball pizza dough, at room temperature
All-purpose flour, for dusting
1 tablespoon coarse cornmeal, for dusting

Preheat oven to 450°F. If using a pizza stone, set it on the middle oven rack for at least 45 minutes to become thoroughly hot. If using a pizza pan or cookie sheet, preheat the oven but not the pan.

Begin by dusting both hands with flour. Turn the ball of dough out onto a lightly floured work surface. With firm fingertips, swiftly press the dough out from the center to the edge while rotating and flattening the circle until it is about 6 inches in diameter. Let dough rest for 10 minutes.

Either roll out the dough with a rolling pin or toss it in the air. If tossing, pick up the dough and stretch and turn it, letting gravity do some of the work and repeating several times until the dough feels floppy. Cup your hands with palms downward and place the backs of your hands under either side of the dough circle; it should drape over

them. Adjust your shoulders so that one hand is in front of the other and, with conviction, turn and twist your hands in a vigorous upward motion. As you toss it, the dough will be bouncing off your knuckles. Keep your eyes on the dough so you don't drop it on the way down. Repeat tossing until the dough circle reaches 12 inches in diameter. If it tears, simply fold the torn edges over each other and pinch to seal the rip. When dough has stretched to the desired size, let it rest for 10 minutes.

Prepare either a pizza peel or a pan by sprinkling evenly with cornmeal. Lift the stretched dough onto the cornmeal and lightly pinch the edges up to create a lip on the crust. Don't worry if it's not a perfect circle; the pizza will taste delicious no matter the shape.

Arrange your favorite toppings (see below for two of OTTO's most popular combinations). If you're using a pizza pan, slide it into the oven, rotating the pan once after 5 minutes and continuing to bake for another 5–6 minutes, or until bottom and edges of the crust are browned.

If you're baking with a pizza stone, use the peel to transfer the pizza carefully onto the top of the hot stone. Position the tip of the peel at the far edge of the stone, tilting it slightly upward. Gently shimmy the peel back toward the oven door, sliding the pizza onto the stone. There should be enough cornmeal on the peel to keep the dough from sticking. After about 5 minutes, rotate the pizza by nosing the peel underneath it to turn. Continue to bake for another 5–6 minutes, or until the bottom and edges of the crust are browned.

When fully baked, slide the pizza out of the pan or place the peel under the pizza to remove it from the stone. Set pizza on a cutting board to cool for 3 minutes before slicing and serving.

MASHED POTATO, BACON & SCALLION PIZZA

(MAKES ONE 12-INCH PIE)

Dough for 12-inch pizza, prepared
 and stretched
Extra virgin olive oil
Freshly ground black pepper
2 tablespoons grated Asiago cheese
1 cup chilled mashed potatoes, skins left on
 and slightly lumpy
1 cup shredded whole-milk mozzarella
¼ cup heavy cream
½ cup cooked, chopped bacon
¼ cup thinly sliced scallions
1 tablespoon finely chopped mixed fresh herbs
 (flat parsley, thyme, rosemary)
Sea salt, to taste

To assemble the pizza: Brush the dough with
extra virgin olive oil and cover lightly with freshly
ground black pepper. Sprinkle Asiago cheese
evenly over the dough. Crumble mashed
potatoes over the dough in an even layer,
keeping potatoes ½ inch from the edge of the
dough. Cover evenly with shredded mozzarella,
then drizzle with heavy cream. Sprinkle with
bacon, scallions, mixed chopped herbs, and sea
salt to taste. Bake as directed above.

Roasted Eggplant & Tomato, Herbed Ricotta & Fresh Basil Pizza

(MAKES ONE 12-INCH PIE)

For the roasted tomatoes:

5 sprigs fresh thyme

1 sprig fresh rosemary

5 whole garlic cloves, peeled

½ cup extra virgin olive oil

2 (35-ounce) cans high-quality whole peeled tomatoes

Sea salt and freshly ground black pepper, to taste

1 medium eggplant, cut in half longitudinally

Extra virgin olive oil, for brushing

Sea salt and freshly ground black pepper, to taste

Dough for 12-inch pizza, prepared and stretched

1 tablespoon finely chopped mixed fresh herbs
   (flat parsley, thyme, rosemary)

½ cup ricotta cheese

2 tablespoons grated Asiago cheese

1 cup shredded whole-milk mozzarella

¼ cup heavy cream

Fresh basil leaves, torn

To make the roasted tomatoes: Preheat oven to 300°F. Gather together fresh thyme and rosemary sprigs and tie with kitchen twine. Set aside. In a 3-inch-deep roasting pan, set over medium-high heat, brown garlic cloves in the olive oil. Add the herb bundle and canned tomatoes to the pan, and season with salt and pepper to taste. Place roasting pan in the oven, uncovered, and bake until most of the liquid is gone and tomatoes begin to brown. Remove from oven and discard herbs and garlic cloves. Roasted tomatoes can be made a day in advance and refrigerated.

To roast the eggplant: Preheat oven to 350°F. Brush cut ends of the eggplant with olive oil and season with salt and freshly ground black pepper. Place on a baking sheet and roast for 30–40 minutes, or until skin becomes crisp but flesh hasn't turned to mush. Remove from oven and cool to room temperature before slicing into thin rounds.

To assemble the pizza: Brush the dough with olive oil and lightly cover with freshly ground black pepper. In a small bowl, mix together chopped herbs and ricotta cheese, seasoning to taste with sea salt. Sprinkle Asiago cheese evenly over the dough, then top with 5–6 roasted eggplant slices. Cover pizza evenly with shredded mozzarella and drizzle with heavy cream. Place small dollops of the ricotta mixture and approximately ½ cup of the roasted tomatoes around the pizza, keeping toppings ½ inch away from the edge of the dough. Sprinkle with sea salt to taste, and bake as directed above.

Paciarino

470 Fore Street
(207) 774-3500
www.paciarino.com
Chef/Owners: Fabiana de Savino and Enrico Barbiero

Opened by Milanese transplants Fabiana de Savino and Enrico Barbiero in 2009, Paciarino—according to de Savino the name means "cozy food, like your grandmother makes"—has quickly developed a following for its simple homemade pastas and sauces, its carefully chosen collection of imported Italian foods, and its warm atmosphere. In a bright and airy space with seating on one side of an archway and the open kitchen on the other, the restaurant has a comfortable, familial feel. Heavy tables and chairs in light wood line the room, abstract art is arranged on muted blue walls, rustic armoires hold jars of pickled onions and peppers, and lighting fixtures are made from upside-down metal colanders. In a window, large wooden rolling pins and pasta rollers are arrayed in an earthenware canister.

The day's offerings, generally a handful of noodles and filled pastas made that morning, are chalked on a slate propped by the counter, where orders are placed before customers seat themselves. For those with questions about the pasta varieties, a small bowl of various shapes of dried pasta sits on a table near the counter. A low-key atmosphere extends to the meal, where children are welcome, Italian pop music plays in the background, and plates of cubed fresh bread are served with dollops of sauce for sopping.

The food is the essence of simplicity: rich tomato sauce cloaking twists of eggy fusilli, or spinach ravioli filled with mild ricotta and bathed in butter and fresh sage. Since they opened, chefs de Savino and Barbiero have packaged their pasta and sauces for takeout, available from a cooler near the counter. Recently they've also begun selling them over the Internet.

The dishes below are two of the restaurant's most popular. For the Salsa di Noci, choose a mild ravioli to let the nutty flavor of the sauce come through. At Paciarino, the Pasta alla Norma is generally served with a short noodle, but feel free to experiment and use your favorite shape. Though it's best in summer with garden fresh tomatoes, eggplants, and basil, it's so addictive that you may find yourself making it in January.

Ravioli alla Salsa di Noci

(SERVES 4–6)

2/3 cup loosely packed fresh bread crumbs
1 cup plus 2 teaspoons whole milk
2/3 pound walnuts
1 clove garlic
Scant 1/2 cup grated Parmigiano Reggiano cheese
1/4 teaspoon marjoram
1/2 cup extra virgin olive oil
Salt, to taste
1 pound cheese ravioli (preferably mild,
   like Paciarino's ricotta and spinach)

In a small bowl, combine the bread crumbs and the milk. Set aside.

Reserving 2 tablespoons for the garnish, place the walnuts in a blender or food processor with the bread and milk mixture, garlic, cheese, and marjoram. Blend until sauce is smooth and creamy, then pour in the oil and season well with salt before blending again. Taste to adjust seasonings. Pour into a bowl and set aside.

Bring a large pot of salted water to a boil and cook ravioli until pasta is al dente. Reserve 1 cup of the pasta water, then drain ravioli, pouring them into a large serving bowl while still dripping slightly with water. Sprinkle a little olive oil over the pasta to prevent sticking. Pour walnut sauce over the ravioli and mix gently.

To serve: Roughly chop remaining walnuts and sprinkle them, with a little shaved Parmigiano Reggiano, over the top for garnish.

Pasta alla Norma

(SERVES 4–6)

1 pound short noodles (like cavatappi, gemelli, or *trofie*)
1/4 cup extra virgin olive oil
2 large cloves garlic, chopped
1 eggplant, peeled and cut into 3/4-inch cubes
2 pints grape or heirloom cherry tomatoes
1 cup loosely packed fresh basil leaves,
   torn or shredded
Salt and pepper, to taste
Whole Pecorino, Parmigiano Reggiano, or
   ricotta salata cheese, to shave at the table

Bring a large pot of salted water to a boil, add noodles, and cook until pasta is al dente. Reserve a ladleful of pasta water and drain noodles.

In a heavy, deep skillet heat the olive oil over medium-low heat. Add the garlic and cook for 3 minutes. Increase heat to medium-high, add the eggplant and tomatoes, and stir to coat vegetables with oil. Season to taste with salt and pepper. Cover the pan tightly and cook, stirring once after 7 minutes. Replace the lid and cook until tomatoes burst and eggplant is tender, about 8 more minutes.

Add drained pasta, reserved cooking water, and fresh basil to the tomato-eggplant sauce and toss for 2 minutes. Serve the pasta in bowls, topped with shaved Pecorino, Parmigiano Reggiano, or ricotta salata.

Pepperclub / Good Egg Café

78 Middle Street
(207) 772-0531
www.pepperclubrestaurant.com
Chef/Owners: Mary Ledue Paine and Edwin Fitzpatrick

A mainstay on Portland's vegetarian scene for more than two decades, Pepperclub and the Good Egg Café occupy a single cheerful corner at the edge of the Old Port. Six mornings a week, the doors open early on the brightly painted interior, and chef/owner Mary Paine serves up "eclectic breakfast," reprising a beloved but now defunct breakfast spot from the 1980s, the Good Egg Café. Reopening at 5 p.m., Pepperclub serves dinner nightly in a casual environment named for jazz musician Art Pepper, painted in funky colors and lit by strings of fairy lights.

Chef Paine describes her menu as "world cuisine," and on a given night, entrees can range from Turkish Lamb and Cranberry Tagine to Roasted Vegetables over Risotto Cakes. Though she serves local meats, poultry, and seafood, she specializes in vegetarian and vegan dishes, with many gluten- and dairy-free options. Her talent, honed over the years, is to make these dishes just as savory and satisfying as everything else on the menu.

Pepperclub's vegan, gluten-free Harvest Vegetable Loaf with Mushroom Gravy and Mashed Potatoes is a prime example: filled with vegetables, herbs, and enough hot sauce to give it a kick, its flavors are complex and, as Chef Paine puts it, "much more than just beans and rice." The recipe below makes two large loaves, enough to serve eight people and have leftovers. If you'd rather, the loaf freezes beautifully; simply bake, allow to cool, wrap in plastic, and freeze. To reheat, bring to room temperature and warm in a 350°F oven until hot.

The Good Egg Café's Wheat and Honey English Muffins are perfect for breakfast or as a base for grilled sandwiches and mini-pizzas. In contrast to most English muffins, they're shaped in squares, a fun touch that also makes them easy to prepare. And unlike many yeast doughs, rising time is minimal and the dough takes no kneading, so muffins can easily be made and served the same morning.

HARVEST VEGETABLE LOAF

(SERVES 6–8 GENEROUSLY)

8 ounces plain tempeh, crumbled

¼ cup cider vinegar

¼ cup gluten-free soy sauce

¼ cup all-natural sweetener (maple syrup,
  brown rice syrup, agave)

1 pound split peas or lentils, cooked,
  1 cup cooking water reserved

1 pound sweet potatoes, peeled, cooked, and mashed

1½ cups cooked short-grain brown rice

¼ cup ground flaxseed

10 ounces spinach, washed and coarsely chopped,
  stems and all

1 yellow onion, peeled and coarsely chopped

2 large carrots, peeled and coarsely chopped

2 ribs celery, coarsely chopped

¼ cup canola or olive oil

¼ cup dried marjoram

¼ cup dried basil

2 tablespoons ground or rubbed dried sage

1 tablespoon kosher salt

1 tablespoon freshly ground black pepper

1 teaspoon hot sauce, or ½ teaspoon cayenne pepper

Preheat oven to 400°F. In a shallow baking dish, combine crumbled tempeh, cider vinegar, gluten-free soy sauce, and sweetener, and bake for 30 minutes.

In a large bowl, mix together cooked split peas or lentils and reserved cooking liquid, mashed sweet potatoes, cooked brown rice, ground flaxseed, chopped fresh spinach, and baked tempeh. Set aside.

In a frying pan over medium heat, sauté onion, carrots, celery, and herbs and spices in canola or olive oil, cooking until vegetables are tender. Pour vegetable mixture into the large bowl with the rest of the ingredients and, using a sturdy wooden spoon or a potato masher, thoroughly combine. Taste and adjust for seasoning.

Preheat oven to 425°F. Lightly grease two large loaf pans or one large casserole and press mixture into prepared pan(s). Smooth top of each loaf before placing in the oven. Bake for 1 hour, until loaves begin to puff a little. Let loaves settle for 30 minutes before serving with Mashed Potatoes and Mushroom Gravy (see recipes on page 138).

Vegan Mashed Potatoes

(SERVES 4–6)

4–6 large Yukon Gold potatoes, peeled and
    cut into large chunks

1 large sweet potato, peeled and cut into
    large chunks

¼ cup canola oil

¼ cup olive oil

2 tablespoons onion powder

1 tablespoon kosher salt

2 teaspoons freshly ground black pepper

In a large pot over medium high heat, boil potatoes and sweet potatoes in enough water to cover by 1 inch. Cook until fork tender, then drain, reserving 1 cup of cooking liquid. Mash potatoes with reserved liquid, oils, onion powder, salt, and pepper. Taste and adjust for seasoning before serving.

Vegan, Gluten-Free Mushroom Gravy

(MAKES 1 QUART)

1 medium yellow onion, coarsely chopped

6 tablespoons canola oil

1 pound mushrooms, cleaned, trimmed, and sliced

¾ cup vegan "Worcestershire sauce" (recipe below)

1 tablespoon freshly ground black pepper

Salt, if needed

3 cups water

¼ cup brown rice flour

In a large skillet over medium-high heat, sauté onions in 2 tablespoons of the canola oil until fragrant and lightly browned. Add mushrooms and continue sautéing until very browned. Stir in vegan "Worcestershire sauce" and pepper, and salt as needed. Add water and bring to a boil.

In a small saucepan, heat the remaining 4 tablespoons of canola oil and whisk in the brown rice flour, cooking to make a roux. Whisk the roux into the boiling gravy to thicken, taste for salt and pepper, and adjust seasonings as desired.

Vegan "worcestershire sauce"

(MAKES 3/4 CUP)

¼ cup cider vinegar

¼ cup gluten-free soy sauce

¼ cup molasses or your favorite sweetener

Combine cider vinegar, gluten-free soy sauce, and molasses or other sweetener. This versatile condiment, which may be made in any quantity and kept on the shelf, will find many uses in the vegan kitchen.

Wheat & Honey English Muffins

(MAKES 15 ENGLISH MUFFINS)

2 cups warm water

2 tablespoons yeast

½ cup honey

1 tablespoon kosher salt

½ cup canola oil

3 cups all-purpose white flour, plus extra for rolling

1½ cups whole wheat flour

¼ cup stone-ground cornmeal

In a large bowl, combine water, yeast and honey. Let proof until yeast is bubbly, about 10 minutes.

To the yeast mixture, add salt, oil, and both flours and stir with a large spoon to combine ingredients. Stir with large strokes, approximately 50 times. The dough will resemble a thick batter rather than bread dough. Let dough rest and rise until doubled in bulk, about ½ hour.

Preheat oven to 400°F. Flour a countertop or other flat work surface. Scrape dough out of the bowl and onto the counter. Sprinkle with more flour and pat the dough into a rectangle approximately 12 x 20 inches. With a sharp knife or dough scraper, cut dough into fifteen 4-inch squares—three rows in one direction and five in the other.

Sprinkle two cookie sheets (or more, depending on size) with cornmeal. Carefully lift squares of dough from the counter with a scraper or metal spatula and place them on the cookie sheets, leaving plenty of space between for muffins to spread and rise.

Bake English muffins in the preheated oven for 1 minute, or until lightly browned. Let muffins cool on the pans before carefully slicing with a serrated knife. Toast and serve immediately with butter and jam, or let cool completely before placing in Ziploc bags and refrigerating or freezing for future use.

PETITE JACQUELINE

190 STATE STREET
(207) 553-7044
WWW.BISTROPJ.COM
CHEF: STEVE CORRY; HEAD SOUS-CHEF: BRANDON RUBLE

With outdoor seating on the brick sidewalk of Longfellow Square, waitstaff in horizontally striped knit shirts and long white aprons, and a menu to please any Francophile, Petite Jacqueline offers classic French bistro cooking in the heart of Portland's West End. Named for chef/owner Steve Corry's ninety-year-old French-born grandmother Jacqueline (who is, in fact, *très petite*), the idea for the bistro came from a trip Corry and his wife and business partner, Michelle (who together own Five Fifty-Five, page 84), took with Jacqueline to France, where they traveled widely, cooking with family and friends and eating at three-star restaurants. Upon their return, the Corrys were inspired to open a casual bistro, serving authentic French dishes in a convivial atmosphere. Petite Jacqueline opened in the spring of 2011, its walls decorated with Jacqueline's old black-and-white photos, family memorabilia, and a few bottles from their well-chosen wine selections. Their motto, etched in glass over a banquette on the back wall, is "Bonne Cuisine, Bonne Cave": Good Food, Good Cellar.

In the kitchen, Chef Corry, Head Sous-Chef Brandon Ruble, and their team turn out the best of bistro cuisine: perfectly dressed greens and composed salads, long-simmering cassoulet, beef bourguignon heady with herbs and wine, garlicky *moules*

with golden *frites*, and for dessert, rich mousse au chocolat and crème caramel. The recipes that follow need only a side of your favorite potatoes to create a bistro meal at home. A word of caution: when making the steak, follow directions exactly and make sure not to overcook. For the steak's sauce, save the Courvoisier for drinking and use an inexpensive brandy; the sauce won't suffer for it. Since the meat cooks so quickly, make your side dishes while the steak marinates, and save cooking the steak until just before serving.

STEAK AU POIVRE

(SERVES 4)

4 (8-ounce) skirt steaks
10 sprigs parsley
6 sprigs thyme
2 cups red wine
Coarsely ground black pepper
1 tablespoon canola oil
4 ounces brandy
4 ounces heavy cream
½ cup (1 stick) unsalted butter
Salt, to taste

Rinse and pat dry the steaks. Coarsely chop the parsley and remove thyme leaves from their stems. Scatter half the herbs in a shallow dish that will accommodate the steaks, and reserve the rest. Pour in wine, add steaks, and marinate for 30 minutes.

Preheat oven to 350°F. Remove steaks from marinade and pat dry. Coat one side of each steak with coarsely ground black pepper. In a large sauté pan over a high flame, heat oil until smoking. Sear steaks, pepper side down, for 3 minutes. Flip steaks and place entire pan in the oven. For medium-rare, cook for 5 minutes. Remove steaks from pan and set aside on a platter to rest.

Drain fat from the pan and place on the stove over medium heat. Deglaze the pan with brandy,

then add heavy cream and cook until mixture is reduced by three-quarters. Whisk butter in until melted, then stir in the remaining parsley and thyme. Taste, and add salt to your preference. Place steaks on four serving plates and spoon sauce over the top.

SALADE D'AUTOMNE

(SERVES 4)

For the dressing:

1 cup (2 sticks) unsalted butter
⅓ cup apple cider
⅓ cup apple cider vinegar
1 small shallot, peeled and diced
1 teaspoon Dijon mustard
⅓ cup maple syrup
Salt, to taste

For the salad:

2 medium red beets
2 tablespoons olive oil
1 sprig thyme

2 heads red leaf lettuce or salad greens of choice
½ cup candied walnuts (see note)
½ cup crumbled blue cheese
1 stalk celery, thinly sliced
Salt, to taste

To make the dressing: Melt butter in a small saucepan over medium heat and cook until light brown. Strain through a fine mesh strainer and set aside. Place remaining ingredients in a blender and process until smooth. Slowly add melted butter to the blender in a thin stream, processing until mixture is fully incorporated. Store dressing at room temperature, and warm before serving.

To roast the beets: Scrub and trim, leaving skin on. Preheat oven to 400°F. Toss beets in olive oil, thyme, and salt, and wrap in two layers of aluminum foil. Roast for 45 minutes or until a fork is easily inserted into the center of the beet. Remove from oven and cool to room temperature before peeling and dicing.

To assemble the salad: Combine prepared beets, lettuce, candied walnuts, blue cheese, and celery in a large salad bowl. Before serving, toss with warmed vinaigrette and salt to taste.

Note: To make candied walnuts: In a small saucepan over medium heat, combine ½ cup water with ½ cup sugar and heat until sugar is dissolved. Add ½ cup walnuts and poach nuts until candied all the way through. The nuts will begin to look translucent as they poach. To test for doneness, remove one, cool, and taste. Strain and let rest until cool. Toss cooled walnuts in 3 tablespoons of sugar. In a large skillet, heat ½ cup vegetable oil to 350°F. Fry candied walnuts until dark brown, then remove from oil and let rest until cool.

MOUSSE AU CHOCOLAT

(SERVES 6)

6¾ ounces dark chocolate
3 tablespoons unsalted butter
5 eggs
6 tablespoons sugar
1½ cups heavy cream

In the top of a double boiler over medium-low heat, melt chocolate and butter until the mixture is slightly warmer than body temperature.

Using the whisk attachment of an electric mixer, beat eggs until foamy.

In a small saucepan, combine 5 tablespoons sugar with just enough water to moisten, and heat over high heat to 240°F.

While sugar mixture is heating, whip heavy cream in a chilled bowl with remaining sugar until soft peaks form. Cover with plastic wrap and refrigerate until ready to use.

With the mixer on medium-high, slowly drizzle cooked sugar into whipped eggs and whisk until bowl feels slightly warm and mixture has doubled in volume, approximately 15 minutes.

Whisk a small amount of the egg mixture into the melted chocolate to temper, followed by a small amount of the whipped cream.

Pour remaining egg mixture into the chocolate, and mix with a spatula. Once these are fully incorporated, fold in remaining whipped cream. Spoon into serving cups and chill to let set overnight before serving.

Ribollita

41 Middle Street
(207) 774-2972
www.ribollitamaine.com
Chef/Owner: Kevin Quiet

One of the earliest upscale Italian restaurants to emerge on Portland's food scene, Chef Kevin Quiet's Ribollita opened in 1996, the product of his love for Italian cuisine and the serendipitous availability of a storefront at the fringe of the Old Port in what was once the city's Little Italy. On a block that now holds some of Portland's most acclaimed restaurants—Hugo's, Duckfat, East Ender—when Ribollita opened, it was virtually alone, across the street from the Jordan's Meats factory (which has since been gutted by fire and demolished). The restaurant space had most recently been a barber shop, and the only trace of Italian food in the vicinity was historic Micucci's, a landmark Italian grocery at the end of the block. Undeterred, Chef Quiet created a small, twelve-table trattoria-inspired restaurant with a menu of classic Italian cooking, steering clear of red sauce to offer veal osso bucco with polenta, handmade ravioli and gnocchi, and the Tuscan vegetable and bread soup after which the restaurant was named.

Over the years, more Italian restaurants have appeared around town, and the neighborhood at the base of Munjoy Hill has been transformed, but Ribollita has stayed a constant, with Chef Quiet's kitchen turning out dishes that incorporate seasonal produce with local seafoods and meats. The Fried Zucchini Blossoms are a summer treat, on the menu only when Chef Quiet can get them from Snell Farm in nearby Buxton. Delicious on their own, Chef Quiet also recommends serving them with a favorite summer sauce; here they're pictured with basil pesto.

FRIED ZUCCHINI BLOSSOMS WITH GOAT CHEESE

(SERVES 6–8)

18 zucchini blossoms
1½ pounds fresh goat cheese
Flour for dredging
3 eggs, lightly beaten
Canola oil for frying

Slice the zucchini blossoms along the side and gently tuck the goat cheese inside the blossoms. Lightly dust the stuffed blossoms with flour, tapping away any excess. Pass the blossoms through the egg wash and back through the flour.

In a large frying pan, heat ½ inch of oil over high heat. When the oil shimmers, gently place the blossoms in the pan and fry, turning once and lightly browning both sides. Place blossoms on paper towels to catch any excess oil. Serve plain, or garnish with a favorite sauce.

ROSEMONT BAKERY AND MARKET

580 BRIGHTON AVENUE
(207) 774-8129

88 CONGRESS STREET
(207) 773-7888

96 MAIN STREET, YARMOUTH
(207) 846-1234
WWW.ROSEMONTMARKET.COM
OWNERS: JOHN NAYLOR AND SCOTT ANDERSON
CHEFS: SCOTT ANDERSON AND ERIN LYNCH

First opened in 2005 in a building that had served as a neighborhood bakery and small grocery under various owners since the 1930s, Rosemont Bakery and Market has been a driving force in the city's local food scene ever since. Specializing in pastries, breads, prepared foods, and upscale pantry staples, Rosemont serves savories and sweets to retail and wholesale customers, and since its inception has expanded to include stores on Munjoy Hill and in the nearby town of Yarmouth. The concept is simple: local produce, cheeses, and meats are displayed with information about their origins; shelves are stocked by owners John Naylor and Scott Anderson with their favorite kitchen goods—from sea salt to steel-cut oats to a wide selection of reasonably priced (and a few extravagant) wines—and refrigerated cases, freezers, and bakery shelves teem with sauces, take-out entrees, breads, and desserts made on-site.

Co-owner and chef Scott Anderson draws on his training at La Varenne Cooking School in Paris to turn out perfect baguettes and croissants from the ovens on Brighton Avenue, still perched on the bakery's original grooved maple flooring. But he and Chef Erin Lynch also cater to the community's taste for humbler fare like sourdough bread and bagels, lasagnas and pot pies, and treats such as Ginger Molasses and Chocolate Stout cakes. The combination has earned them a loyal following, made more so by their relationships with local producers and the company's ambition to educate customers on the origins of their food.

The Chicken Pot Pie below is a fantastic way to use up leftover roasted chicken; depending on your preference, you can use white meat, dark meat, or a combination of the two. Chefs Anderson and Lynch use pasture-raised chickens from Mainely Poultry, a family-owned farm in Warren, and make their stock from the leftover bones, skin, and drippings of the roasted chicken for the filling. You'll have enough filling for two pies, but if you want to make only one, you can freeze it for later use. For each pie, you'll need dough for a 9-inch two-crust pie.

CHICKEN POT PIE

(MAKES TWO 9-INCH PIES)

Half a roasted chicken (any half—white, dark,
   or a combination)
3 tablespoons unsalted butter
¾ pound mushrooms, sliced
4 stalks celery, diced
¼ pound carrots, diced
4 tablespoons flour
2 sprigs fresh sage, chopped
2½ cups chicken stock, if possible made from
   the roasted chicken above
1 scant cup organic peas
Salt and freshly ground black pepper
Dough for 2 two-crust 9-inch pies (homemade
   from your favorite recipe, or Rosemont's frozen
   All-Butter Pastry)

Pull the meat from the roasted chicken and shred
it. If you can, make a stock by simmering the
bones, skin, and drippings from the roast.

To make the filling: In a deep skillet or Dutch
oven, melt butter over medium-high heat. Add
mushrooms, celery, and carrots and sauté
until tender. Sprinkle flour over the vegetables
and continue sautéing for 1 minute, stirring
continuously. Add sage and stock, and simmer
to thicken. Stir in chicken shreds and peas and
season with salt and pepper to taste. Cool filling
to room temperature.

To assemble the pies: Preheat oven to 350°F.
Divide dough into four pieces and roll out on
a lightly floured surface. For each pie, press a
round of dough into a pie tin. Pour filling into
prepared pie tin and cover with a second round

of rolled-out dough. Tuck edges under and pinch
top and bottom crusts together to seal. Cut
vents in the top crust, and bake until the pastry is
golden and the filling bubbles through the vents.

SAFARI

30 Washington Avenue
(207) 773-1008
Chef/Owner: Hinda Hassan

When Somali-born Hinda Hassan took over the space that had housed Hamdi, a restaurant and market that catered to Portland's African community, she had two goals in mind: she wanted to keep the family-friendly halal business going, and she wanted to expand its menu to attract a wider clientele. Changing the name to Safari, she broadened the offerings to include dishes from all regions of Africa. Beneath murals of giraffes and elephants roaming the grassy plains, Safari now serves foods from across the continent, from Kenyan stews to Moroccan falafel to Somali roasted goat. The attached grocery sells staples of the African kitchen—imported grains, oils, beans, and spices—bringing in customers from the city's Somali community, while the new menu has found fans around town.

The falafel below is exceptionally moist and creamy on the inside, with a crisp outer shell. Herb and spice measurements are approximate, so feel free to adjust to your taste; Chef Hassan recommends frying one falafel first as a test and tasting for seasoning before cooking the entire batch. At Safari, Hassan serves falafel with a simple chopped salad of lettuce, tomato, and cilantro, accompanied by tahini sauce and, in a quirky twist, a drizzle of ranch dressing.

Safari's Falafel

(SERVES 4–6)

For falafel:

1 pound dried chickpeas
3–4 cloves garlic, chopped
Small bunch of cilantro, chopped
2–3 tablespoons ground cumin
½ teaspoon salt, or more to taste
Vegetable oil for frying

For tahini sauce:

½ cup tahini
Juice of ½ lime
Salt to taste
Water

In a large pot, soak chickpeas overnight in enough water to cover by 3 inches. When ready to cook, drain beans, cover again with cold water, and bring to a boil, simmering for 45 minutes or until soft. Drain beans, and when cool enough to handle, pulse them in a food processor with garlic, cilantro, cumin, and salt, processing them until creamy.

In a heavy, deep skillet, heat 1 inch of oil to 350°F. Using a soup spoon or a small ice cream scoop, measure a golf-ball-sized amount of the chickpea mixture and use your hands to shape into a smooth ball. Fry in the oil for 5 minutes, flipping or rolling the falafel to make sure it's crisp on all sides, then drain excess oil on a paper towel.

While falafels are frying, whisk together tahini, lime juice, and ⅛ teaspoon salt in a small bowl. The mixture will be very thick. Add water by teaspoonfuls until you reach desired consistency, adjusting lime juice and salt to taste.

Serve falafel with tahini sauce, ranch dressing, and a simple chopped salad.

MAINE SODAS, OLD AND NEW

In the tradition of Maine's iconic Moxie soda, a bittersweet brew created by Union's Dr. Augustin Thompson in 1884, a new wave of nonalcoholic beverages has swept the state. Begun with Maine Root, an organic, fair-trade-certified soda, there are now several companies crafting artisan sodas around the state. Maine Root bottles its original root beer, as well as ginger beer, sarsaparilla, and blueberry and orange sodas. Green Bee makes its Lemon Sting with honey, lemon, and rosemary, and has recently launched Blueberry Dream, made from wild blueberries and honey. Capt'n Eli's, brewed by beer makers Shipyard Brewing Company, includes Strawberry Pop and Parrot Punch among its classic offerings. And of course, Moxie can still be found bottled or in the bright orange can. Try them all on tap at restaurants around Portland, or pick up a four-pack at groceries around the state.

The Salt Exchange

245 Commercial Street
(207) 347-5687
www.thesaltexchange.net
Chef: Adam White Jr.
Owners: Charles and Martha Bryon

When newlyweds Charles and Martha Bryon first began dreaming of a professional collaboration, they gravitated toward the arts, imagining a gallery that would showcase local visual artists. As they talked more about the project, however, they realized that their joint passion for food was itself an art, and their focus shifted to what would become The Salt Exchange: a restaurant that "celebrates art, contemporary American cuisine, and sincere hospitality."

Past a swinging slate gray sign and green pillars in an old brick building on Commercial Street, the Bryons opened the restaurant in 2009, with an emphasis on shareable small plates, creative cocktails, and a deep list of wines and bourbons. True to their original plan, the walls are adorned with changing collections from local artists, light filters through custom-made stained glass windows, and a warm cherrywood bar, the creation of a professor at Maine College of Art, overlooks the open kitchen. Chef Adam White Jr. joined the restaurant soon after opening, bringing an eclectic background—a degree in engineering from Northeastern University, a commitment to

community involvement, three decades cooking everywhere from Maine to Atlanta to Montechiari, Italy—and a varied palate to the menu. His seasonally changing menu can be deceptively simple, but it's dotted with surprises: braised shortribs are paired with candied brussels sprouts; briny Glidden Point oysters are accompanied by lemon sorbet.

When making Chef White's Poached Lobster, keep in mind that you'll need to begin by making a lobster stock. This versatile stock will keep, refrigerated, for one week, or can be frozen for later use. Once the stock is made, assembling the dish is simple, and its combination of earthy root vegetables, sweet leeks and lobster, and smoky bacon makes an impressive and satisfying dish for guests. Both lobster shells for the stock and cooked, shelled lobster meat for the finished dish can generally be found at your local fish market.

Poached Lobster

(SERVES 4)

1 cup peeled, diced, and blanched carrots

1 cup peeled, diced, and blanched potatoes

½ cup leeks, white part only, sliced and well rinsed

½ cup bacon, crisped, drained, and chopped

2 cups lobster stock (recipe below)

1 sprig fresh thyme

¼ cup heavy cream

4 lobster tails, cooked and shelled

4 lobster claws, cooked and shelled

Salt and pepper to taste

Chopped fresh flat leaf parsley, for garnish

In a medium saucepan, combine carrots, potatoes, leeks, bacon, and lobster stock, and bring to a simmer. Add the thyme sprig, cream, and lobster, warming lobster thoroughly, about 2 minutes. Be careful not to overcook the lobster, as it will toughen. Remove from heat and discard thyme. Adjust seasonings to taste.

To serve: Divide carrots, potatoes, leeks, bacon, and broth equally among four serving bowls. Add 1 lobster tail and 1 claw to each bowl. Garnish with a sprinkle of parsley.

Lobster Stock

(MAKES 1 QUART)

3 pounds lobster shells

2 gallons water

½ yellow onion, peeled and coarsely chopped

1 carrot, peeled and chopped

1 stalk celery, washed and chopped

1 sprig fresh thyme

1 clove garlic

1 bay leaf

3 black peppercorns

1 tablespoon tomato paste

In a large stockpot, combine all ingredients. Bring to a boil over medium-high heat, then reduce to a simmer. Simmer, uncovered, for 1 hour. Remove from heat and strain stock, discarding solids. Return stock to the pot and simmer until reduced by half. Strain again and transfer to a storage container. Refrigerate until needed. Stock will keep for 1 week in the refrigerator.

LOBSTAH

In the popular imagination, nothing says Maine more than boiled lobster: steaming hot, scarlet from the boiling pot, served with a cup of drawn butter, corn on the cob, a handful of potato chips, and a bib. It's taken the humble lobster a while, however, to achieve this iconic status. Long a staple in the diet of Maine's Native American population, lobsters were initially considered a "poor man's protein" by European settlers because of their abundance. They were fed to apprentices, indentured servants, and prisoners for more than a century, and it wasn't until the late 1800s that the crustacean began to be considered a delicacy. Now, the waters off the coastline are dotted with brightly colored buoys—each pattern distinctive so that fishermen can find their traps—and no visit to Maine is considered complete without at least one lobster dinner, preferably seated near the water on a pier near a lobster pound.

Schulte & Herr

349 Cumberland Avenue
(207) 773-1997
http://schulteundherr.wordpress.com/
Chef/Owner: Brian Davin; Co-Owner: Steffi Davin

Off the beaten path, down a quiet side street west of Congress, a sign on a white clapboard building reads "Schulte & Herr, breakfast • lunch." On a sandwich board propped beneath the springy green awning, the owners clarify: Homemade German Food. Opened the same weekend Hurricane Irene struck Portland, in a space that was formerly the home of a series of Southeast Asian restaurants, Schulte & Herr is the product of the chef/owner team Brian and Steffi Davin. Chef Davin, a graduate of the

New England Culinary Institute in Montpelier, spent years cooking in Europe before meeting his German wife, Steffi, and settling in Berlin. After nearly a decade there, the couple moved to the States, bringing with them a passion for home-style German food prepared with a deft hand. Appropriately, they named the restaurant after their respective families' maternal lines—Schulte was Steffi's mother's maiden name, and Herr was the maiden name of Brian's great-grandmother, who came to America from Germany.

In this unassuming cafe, seating fewer than twenty under the framed woodcuts on its walls, customers feast on crisp potato pancakes with house-cured lox, horseradish, and capers, or creamy spaetzle under melted Emmenthal cheese on a bed of caramelized onions. Breads are homemade and served with small pots of Liptauer cheese; artisan sausages and smoked hams come from Maurice Bonneau's Sausage Kitchen in Lisbon Falls. The changing desserts range from apple strudel to rich homemade vanilla custard topped with seasonal fruit compote—spiced plums, pumpkins poached in maple syrup—comfort food at its most glorious.

With so few ingredients, the key to success with the recipes below is to use the best possible: fresh herbs, farm eggs, and top-quality cheese. Before you begin, make sure your kitchen is equipped with a potato ricer for pressing the spaetzle, available in the gadget section of most kitchen stores.

Swabian Spaetzle with Caramelized Onions & Emmenthal Cheese

(SERVES 6)

For the dough:

4 cups all-purpose flour

4 eggs

1 cup water

1 teaspoon salt

Freshly grated nutmeg

Vegetable oil

3 medium yellow onions

4 tablespoons unsalted butter

½ pound Emmenthal cheese, grated

Chopped fresh chives, for garnish

To make the spaetzle, in a large bowl, mix together flour, eggs, water, salt, and nutmeg, kneading the mixture until dough is smooth.

Bring a large pot of salted water to a boil over high heat, then reduce heat to medium-high so that water stays at a simmer. Place a ladleful of dough into a potato ricer and press dough directly into simmering water. In a short moment, spaetzle will begin to float to the surface. Cook for about 1 minute, until they look puffy. Using a slotted spoon or strainer, take the spaetzle out of the pot and place them in a bowl of ice water. Continue, working in batches, until all the dough has been cooked. Strain spaetzle in a colander and drizzle with a little vegetable oil to prevent sticking.

Peel onions and slice into ¼-inch rings. Pour enough vegetable oil into a large skillet to cover the bottom with a thin film. Heat over a medium-high burner, add the onions, and fry until golden brown. Remove onions from the pan and set aside.

In the same large skillet, melt butter, pour in drained spaetzle, and sauté until brown, approximately 2 minutes. Reduce the heat to low and add the cooked onions. Stir the spaetzle, sprinkling the grated cheese into them. Once the cheese has browned, the spaetzle are ready. Serve with a sprinkle of chopped chives and a cucumber salad.

Cucumber Salad with Fresh Dill

(SERVES 4)

For the dressing:

3 tablespoons canola oil

2 tablespoons red wine vinegar

Pinch of salt

Pinch of black pepper

Pinch of sugar

2 European cucumbers, peeled and thinly sliced

2 tablespoons chopped fresh dill

In a medium bowl, whisk together all dressing ingredients. Add cucumbers and chopped dill, stirring to combine. Chill until ready to serve.

Silly's Restaurant

40 Washington Avenue
(207) 772-0360
www.sillys.com
Chef/Owner: Colleen Kelley

A Portland landmark since it opened in 1988, Silly's began as an outlet for Deirdre and Stephanie Nice to sell their signature Fast Abdullahs, wraps stuffed with everything from veggies (Tempeh Thru the Tulips) to house-made pork/lamb sausage (the Greatest American Gyro). Bought by current chef/owner Colleen Kelley in 2002, the restaurant has since branched out, adding table service and a radically expanded menu. But the quirkily named dishes, retro vibe—Formica tables, vintage ceramic salt and pepper shakers, towering old-fashioned layer cakes—and general good feeling of the place have kept visitors entertained and regulars loyal.

On display inside the white clapboard storefront, lunchboxes and T-shirts bearing Silly's logo and a quote from Albert Einstein next to a cartoon of his face read "As far as we can discern, the universe is a very silly place," while the walls are filled to the ceiling with framed photos taken around the world of patrons holding "Eat at Silly's" bumper stickers. The photos have been accumulating since the Nice sisters moved into the space, and Chef Kelley recalls a customer tearing up to see a picture high on the wall of himself as a child with his father, who had recently passed away. While she rotates some of the pictures, Chef Kelley doesn't touch the older ones, or those of service members.

Building community and giving back to the neighborhood are important to Chef Kelley, and her service ranges from accommodating gluten-free and vegan patrons to sponsoring public radio to bringing the hand truck out of the cellar to help neighbors take their clothes to the laundromat. Silly's is a frequent winner of "best service" awards, and in 2011 was named the "Flavor of Portland" in the Independent Business Awards.

Having grown up in her parents' restaurant, Chef Kelley has kept Silly's a family affair and her retired dad, John, stays busy smoking pork and prepping ingredients a few days a week. Her sister, Shelley Kelley, bought the building next door to expand seating and offer a full bar, continuing Silly's sisterly history.

A menu favorite, fried pickles are crinkle cut, dipped in spicy batter, and fried to golden perfection. The batter is versatile—Silly's uses it for their Rings of Fire (fried jalapeños), and for fried green tomato and fried cheese stick specials, and though it calls for buttermilk, the batter can be made vegan by substituting pickle juice for the dairy. Both masa harina and sambal oelek chili paste can be found in the international section of most groceries.

Bunchy's Lemon Drop Cake is made from an old recipe of Chef Kelley's mother, whose nickname is Honeybunch. The recipe makes enough for one three-layer cake, and a single six-inch layer. In the Kelley family, the six-inch cake is called a Big John cake, after Chef Kelley's father; at the restaurant, the layer is still frosted and set aside for Big John. While the amount of Cream Cheese Frosting may seem surprising, Chef Kelley says not to skimp: "good frosting to cake ratio is a priority here at Silly's."

FRIED PICKLES WITH SPICY SAUCE

(SERVES 4–6)

For the pickles:

1½ cups all-purpose flour
2 cups corn flour (masa harina)
⅓ cup garlic powder
4 teaspoons cayenne pepper
¼ cup chili powder
2 cups crinkle-cut dill pickle slices
   (approximately one 16-ounce jar)
2 cups buttermilk
Canola oil, for frying

For the sauce:

1 cup mayonnaise
2 tablespoons sambal oelek chili paste
1 tablespoon freshly squeezed lemon juice

To make the fried pickles: In a large bowl whisk together flour, corn flour, garlic powder, cayenne pepper, and chili powder. Take pickles out of their jar and dry briefly on paper towels. Dip in buttermilk, then dredge in flour mixture. Using a colander or a wire basket, shake off the excess batter.

In a deep pot over high heat, bring several inches of canola oil to 350°F. Working in batches, fry pickles until golden brown, 2–3 minutes. Place on paper towels to soak up excess oil.

To make the sauce: Whisk together mayonnaise, chili paste, and lemon juice. Taste to adjust seasoning. Serve fried pickles hot with a ramekin of dipping sauce.

Bunchy's Lemon Drop Cake

(MAKES ONE 3-LAYER 10-INCH CAKE AND ONE 6-INCH LAYER)

For the cake:

¹⁄₃ cup unsalted butter, cut into cubes and softened

½ cup shortening

3 cups sugar

6 egg whites, at room temperature

2 whole eggs, at room temperature

2²⁄₃ cups buttermilk, at room temperature

4 cups all-purpose flour

2 teaspoons baking powder

1 teaspoon baking soda

½ teaspoon salt

2 tablespoons lemon extract

For the frosting:

1 pound salted butter, at room temperature

2 pounds cream cheese, at room temperature

8 cups confectioners' sugar

2 tablespoons pure vanilla extract

Crystallized ginger, thinly sliced, for garnish

To make the cake: Preheat oven to 350°F. Lightly grease and flour three 10 x 2-inch cake pans, and one 6 x 2-inch cake pan. Be careful not to overgrease or the cake will sink.

In a large bowl, on the medium speed of a mixer, beat together softened butter, shortening, and sugar until light and fluffy.

In a separate bowl, whip together egg whites, eggs, and buttermilk. In yet another bowl, sift together flour, baking powder, baking soda, and salt.

Alternating wet and dry mixtures, add them to the butter mixture, beating until just incorporated (do not overmix). Add the lemon extract and beat, scraping down the sides to make sure all ingredients are combined.

Pour batter into prepared 10-inch pans, filling them two-thirds full. Do not overfill, or the cake won't bake through. Scrape leftover batter into the 6-inch "Big John" cake pan. Bake in preheated oven for 20 minutes, then gently rotate the pans. After 30 minutes in the oven (20 for the Big John cake), press the middle of the cake, and if it springs back, it's done. If not, test again at 5-minute intervals. When done, the cake should be golden brown, and a toothpick inserted into the center should come out with visible crumbs. (Don't wait until it pulls away from the sides, or it will be overbaked.)

Remove from oven and let cakes cool in the pans on a wire rack for 10 minutes. Invert onto cooling racks, remove from pans, and cool thoroughly before icing.

Tip: If you've overgreased the pans and the cakes happen to fall, ice them anyway and fill the indentation with macerated fruit or berries. As Chef Kelley says, "It will still look pretty and taste fantastic! And someone will think you are genius!"

To make the cream cheese frosting: Beat butter in a bowl with a hand mixer until soft and creamy, about 3 minutes. In a large mixing bowl, beat cream cheese until smooth, about 3 minutes. Add butter to the cream cheese and beat on the medium speed of a mixer until fluffy. Gradually add the confectioners' sugar and vanilla, beating until well incorporated.

Cover the bowl of frosting with plastic wrap and refrigerate for at least 30 minutes, making sure the frosting is firm enough to spread smoothly but not so hard that it tears the cake.

To assemble the cake: Put a smear of frosting on the cake stand so that the bottom layer won't slide. Ice between each layer and on the sides and top, reserving 1 cup of frosting for the Big John layer. Decorate the top with thinly sliced crystallized ginger. Use remaining frosting to ice sides and top of the Big John cake. Chill cakes for 1 hour to set frosting. Remove from refrigerator and serve at room temperature.

Sonny's

83 Exchange Street
(207) 772-7774
www.sonnysportland.com
Chef de Cuisine/Owner: Jay Villani
Minister of Flavor: Johnny Walker

Ten years after opening the immensely popular Local 188 (page 110), Chef Jay Villani turned his palate from the Old World to the New with Sonny's, a bar and lounge in the heart of the Old Port. Taking its name from Chef Villani's affectionate nickname for his son, Sonny's is housed in a meticulously restored historic building from the mid-1800s. The restaurant space was formerly the Portland Savings Bank, and it retains the bank's spacious feel, burnished wood, and mosaic floors. What's new are the deep couches, booth seating, and immense glass vats of infused liquor that line the bar.

The food continues the farm-to-table commitment that Chef Villani began at Local 188, but here the flavors lean south, influenced by the cuisines of Brazil, Mexico, Venezuela, and the American Southwest. A meal might include a Tri-Pork Cubano,

layered on house-made bread and served with the restaurant's own pickles, or a Caribbean Fish Stew, combining the catch of the day with a coconut curry broth. Cocktails are novel and cleverly named, combining house-infused liquors—chili-infused tequila, thyme lemon zest vodka, spring strawberry rhubarb vodka—with fresh citrus and muddled herbs.

The vodka infusions below make enough for a crowd—perfect for a party or, decanted into smaller bottles, for a festive gift. If you're planning a smaller gathering, or just want to have a bottle on hand, simply divide the recipe by four.

When making arepas, you must use precooked cornmeal (the package will say *precocida*), available at any Latin grocery or in the specialty aisle of most supermarkets. The recipe won't work with regular cornmeal, no matter how finely ground, or with masa harina, a staple of Mexican cooking made from corn steeped in lime before grinding. In traditional Venezuelan cooking, arepas are cut three-quarters through, hollowed out, and stuffed with a favorite filling. At Sonny's, they like to leave them intact for a more substantial bite, and they cook them with whatever special

they're running (as pictured, the arepa is filled with roasted pork butt, salsa verde, and melted manchego). Keep in mind, as Chef Villani says, "There are no rules when it comes to accompaniments. The arepa is meant to be a vehicle for creativity."

Perfect Pairing

STRAWBERRY RHUBARB VODKA INFUSION

4 quarts strawberries, washed and hulled
2½ pounds rhubarb
4 (750-milliliter) bottles premium vodka (not flavored)

Cut strawberries into quarters and chop rhubarb into ½-inch slices. Put fruit into a large nonreactive pot with a lid and fill with vodka. Fruit should be entirely covered. Let sit at room temperature for up to a week, stirring once daily to help infusion process. After a week, strain and rebottle.

THYME LEMON ZEST VODKA INFUSION

6 lemons
3 healthy sprigs fresh thyme
4 (750-milliliter) bottles premium vodka (not flavored)

Scrub the lemons and cut off tops and bottoms. Thinly slice off the rinds, being careful not to get any of the white pith—all you want is the yellow skin. Put lemon zest and thyme sprigs into a large infusion tank or a nonreactive pot with a lid and fill with vodka. Let sit at room temperature for up to a week, stirring once daily to help infusion process. Strain before serving.

Johnny's Venezuelan Corn Bread

AREPA

(MAKES 8–12 AREPAS)

2 cups milk
2 cups precooked cornmeal
2 teaspoons kosher salt
½ cup brown sugar
½ cup shredded cheddar cheese
   (more if you like cheesy)
Vegetable oil or butter for frying

In a small saucepan over low heat, warm the milk. In a large bowl, combine cornmeal, salt, sugar, and cheese and mix well. Slowly add warm milk to the dry mixture, working dough constantly until it's pliable and neither too dry nor too wet.

Preheat oven to 350°F. Lightly grease a skillet or sauté pan and set it over medium heat. Take a handful of dough and shape it into a patty about ¾ inch thick. If cracks appear at the edges of the round, the dough is too dry and needs a little more liquid. Fry arepas until each side is browned, then place in the oven for 10 minutes. Enjoy with your favorite filling, or simply plain and warm.

Taco Escobarr

548 Congress Street
(207) 541-9097
www.tacoescobarr.com
Chef: Steve Tuggle
Owners: Matt Moran, Jason Loring, Tom Barr 3rd,
Tobey Moulton

In a storefront across the street from their flagship Nosh Kitchen Bar (page 120), the men who brought bacon dust to Portland have turned their palates south. Serving Mexican food in several incarnations—*carne* being the operative word—Taco Escobarr's focus is on tacos and burritos, excellent cocktails, and a smattering of sides (Los Sidekicks). *Jefe de cocina* Steve Tuggle's tacos are served in one of three shells: soft corn tortillas, crispy corn tortilla shells, and the house specialty, "puffy tacos" in deep-fried corn tortillas. Fillings include beef picadillo, carne asado, braised pork, and braised chicken, and toppings are simple onion, cilantro, cheese, and tomato. At the bar, manager and co-owner Tobey Moulton's intense cocktails pack a punch.

The restaurant's aesthetic leans heavily toward Mexican wrestlers and bright Spanish-language B-movie posters, a vibrant look that matches the energy of the staff and the food. As at Nosh, the *diablo* is in the details: fish tacos, another favorite, are made with locally caught pollack and served with house-pickled

slaw, and tortillas are made by hand daily. Chef Tuggle's varied career began in the kitchen of his grandparents' restaurant in Meridian, Texas, and included stints as personal chef to several of the Green Bay Packers. When he landed in Portland, it all came together, and the results—spice, abundance, and cheer—couldn't be more satisfying.

The recipe for La Paloma makes a single generous cocktail, but can easily be multiplied for a crowd. For the Roasted Lobster with Chipotle Mayonnaise, keep in mind that you'll be starting with live lobsters. To split a lobster, Chef Tuggle recommends placing it top side up on a cutting board or counter, holding down the claws (bands still on) with one hand, and slicing down the middle with kitchen shears or a sharp knife.

ROASTED LOBSTER WITH CHIPOTLE MAYONNAISE

1¼ cups extra virgin olive oil
2 large heads garlic, cloves separated, peeled, and minced
2 large egg yolks
4 tablespoons freshly squeezed lime juice
3 canned chipotle peppers (or more for a spicier sauce), chopped
1 teaspoon salt

2 live lobsters, 1¼ pounds each
2 teaspoons extra virgin olive oil

8 ounces mixed salad greens
Lime juice and extra virgin olive oil, to taste
1 lime, sliced into wedges

To make the chipotle mayonnaise: Warm olive oil in a skillet over low heat. Add minced garlic and "sweat" it in the oil. When garlic begins to brown, remove pan from heat and allow to cool. Place egg yolks and lime juice in the bowl of a food processor and, with the motor running, slowly drizzle cooled oil into yolks until the mixture emulsifies. Using a rubber scraper, transfer to a bowl and mix in the chilies and salt. Set aside.

Split the lobsters in half, head to tail. Preheat the broiler. Set a large skillet over medium-high heat and add olive oil to the pan. Place lobsters in the pan, shell side down, until they turn red, then flip them over. Move the pan under the broiler for 2–3 minutes. Flip the lobsters again. Slather chipotle mayonnaise onto the meat side and put back under the broiler until golden brown.

To serve: Arrange greens on a platter and drizzle with fresh lime juice and olive oil. Place lobsters on top and serve with remaining mayonnaise and slices of lime.

Perfect Pairing...

La Paloma Cocktail

(SERVES 1)

3 ounces Sauza Hornitos tequila
1 ounce grapefruit puree
Splash of cranberry juice
1 ounce sour salt (citric acid powder)
1 ounce sugar
Citrus soda
1 slice grapefruit

In a cocktail shaker, combine tequila, grapefruit puree, and cranberry juice with a generous scoop of ice. Shake "till it hurts." On a small plate, mix together sour salt and sugar. Moisten the rim of the glass and dip in the mixture. Pour tequila, juice and ice into the cocktail glass, top with citrus soda, and garnish with a slice of grapefruit.

Serve in a 14-ounce cocktail glass.

THE ROOMS: THE FRONT ROOM, THE GRILL ROOM & THE CORNER ROOM

THE FRONT ROOM RESTAURANT & BAR
73 CONGRESS STREET
(207) 773-3366

THE GRILL ROOM RESTAURANT & BAR
84 EXCHANGE STREET
(207) 774-BEEF (2333)

THE CORNER ROOM KITCHEN & BAR
110 EXCHANGE STREET
(207) 879-4747

WWW.THEFRONTROOMRESTAURANT.COM
CHEF/OWNER: HARDING LEE SMITH

As a late teen, Maine native Harding Lee Smith left the state to pursue his education, earning a degree from Boston University before heading west to attend the Culinary Institute of America in Napa Valley. After years away, cooking everywhere from Italy to Maui, he was lured home by "family and the Red Sox," and the rest is history.

Beginning with his flagship The Front Room restaurant on Munjoy Hill, opened in 2005, Chef Smith's trio of restaurants, collectively called The Rooms, have earned acclaim and a loyal following for their classic dishes, made with local ingredients and priced reasonably enough to encourage customers to become regulars. The Front Room, serving "New American comfort food," offers a menu that ranges from cedar-planked salmon with artichoke–sweet potato hash to that most comforting of comfort foods, Franks & Maple Beans with brown bread. The Grill Room, Chef Smith's second restaurant, is an "urban steakhouse" on the Old Port's busy Exchange Street, marked by a swinging brass sign depicting a bull. Inside, the reclaimed elmwood tables and booths pair nicely with a menu of grilled local meats and wood-fired pizza. The Corner Room, Chef Smith's most recent addition, is housed in a building that formerly held the gallery of the Salt Institute for Documentary Studies, at the top of Exchange Street, and features rustic Italian-inspired dishes served in an open space with high ceilings, large windows, and an open kitchen and visible pasta-making station.

In the recipes below, Chef Smith uses slow braising to bring out the flavors in both beef shortribs and confit of duck leg. In each recipe, the meat becomes so tender that it falls from the bone. Once cooked, the Braised Beef Shortribs can be served either on their own or shredded and incorporated into a ragù, served over homemade gnocchi. The same is true for the duck leg confit—it's delicious solo, and even more so in a ragù with polenta and seared duck breast.

Shortrib Ragù with Potato Gnocchi

(SERVES 8)

Olive oil

2 yellow onions, diced

1 head celery, diced

1 large carrot, diced

Meat from 5 pounds braised bone-in shortribs, shredded (recipe to the right)

Reserved braising juices from shortribs

2 sprigs rosemary

1 bunch sage

2 bay leaves

2 tablespoons unsalted butter

2 pounds gnocchi, cooked (recipe to the right)

Grated Parmigiano Reggiano, for sprinkling

In a large, deep-sided Dutch oven, warm a splash of olive oil over medium-low heat. Add onions and sweat until soft. Add celery and carrots, and continue to sweat until vegetables are soft. Stir in the shortrib meat and enough reserved braising juices to just cover the meat. Tie the rosemary, sage, and bay leaf in a bundle with kitchen twine and add to the pot. Simmer until the mixture is thickened to the consistency of heavy cream.

In a large sauté pan over medium heat, melt butter with a little olive oil and add cooked gnocchi. Gently brown the gnocchi in the pan. Add ragù a little at a time until you have coated the gnocchi well. To serve, spoon into bowls and top with grated cheese.

BRAISED BEEF SHORTRIBS

(SERVES 6)

3 pounds beef shortribs, bone in (preferably 6 corner pieces from the butcher)

Oil for browning

3 carrots, peeled and chopped

1 large onion, peeled and chopped

½ bunch celery, chopped

3 cloves garlic, chopped

1 bottle rich red wine

1 gallon (approximately) beef stock

6 sprigs fresh thyme

Preheat oven to 350°F. In a large Dutch oven over medium heat, brown the shortribs, beginning with fat side down, until well browned on all three sides; this will take about 4–5 minutes per batch. When browned, remove ribs from pan and spoon out and discard the fat. Add a bit of oil and the vegetables, and brown well. Once the vegetables are browned, return ribs to the pan and add wine. Cover bones with stock and bring all to a simmer. Add thyme sprigs and cover with a tight-fitting lid.

Place pot in the oven and braise 1½ hours. Remove lid and continue to cook for 1½ hours more, basting and turning the ribs occasionally.

Remove ribs from oven and cool in the juices in the pan for several hours or overnight.

To serve: Remove meat from bones, carefully removing excess fat and tough pieces. Strain the sauce, discarding vegetables. Warm the meat in the strained juices, either on the stove or in the oven. Good accompaniments include mashed potatoes and vinegar cabbage, and a little horseradish on top.

Using your fingers, make a well in the center of the potato-flour mixture. Crack the eggs into the well and mix the eggs with your fingers while slowly bringing in flour from the edge of the bowl. Once you have a rough mass, remove to a lightly floured countertop and gently knead until the mass comes together into a soft dough. Cover with a kitchen towel and let rest.

Using a sharp knife, divide the dough into five equal pieces. Using your palms, gently roll each piece while moving hands apart from each other until you have a cigar-shaped log. Cut each log into 1-inch pieces. Dust gnocchi with flour and transfer to a cookie sheet.

Bring a large pot of salted water to a boil. Have ready a large bowl of ice water to cool the cooked gnocchi.

Slip gnocchi into the pot. They'll sink at first, but float when done. Allow to sit in pot for 30 seconds, then remove with a slotted spoon or sieve and transfer to the bowl of ice water. Allow gnocchi to cool before straining, then toss with olive oil to keep them from sticking together. Refrigerate cooled gnocchi until ready to use.

POTATO GNOCCHI

(SERVES 8)

2 pounds Russet potatoes, baked, peeled,
    and riced or passed through a food mill
1 cup all-purpose flour, plus extra for dusting
Kosher salt, to taste
2 large eggs

Put potatoes in a large bowl, and if they're still warm from baking, allow to cool. Add flour to the bowl with a couple pinches of salt. Toss the potatoes gently with the flour until mixture is well combined.

Duck Ragù with Pan-Roasted Breast & Parmesan Polenta

(SERVES 4–8, DEPENDING ON THE REST OF THE MEAL)

2 whole ducks

For the duck leg confit:

Legs from the 2 ducks
1 pound brown sugar
1 cup salt
1 tablespoon juniper berries
1 tablespoon fennel seed
1 tablespoon chili flakes
1 head garlic, roughly chopped
1 tablespoon black peppercorns
½ tablespoon ground cardamom

For the duck stock:

Carcasses from the 2 ducks
1 large yellow onion
3 stalks celery
1 large carrot
1 head garlic
2 bay leaves
1 tablespoon black peppercorns

For the duck ragù:

2 cups dried porcini mushrooms
Vegetable oil
1 large yellow onion
1 tablespoon chopped raw garlic
2 cups chopped canned tomatoes
3 cups red wine
Shredded meat from the duck leg confit
Salt and freshly ground black pepper, to taste

Breasts from the 2 ducks
Salt and freshly ground black pepper, to taste

For the polenta:

1 pound instant polenta
2 cups grated Parmesan or other hard cheese
3 tablespoons butter
Salt and freshly ground black pepper, to taste

Using a sharp boning knife, remove legs and breasts from each duck. Reserve the breasts in the refrigerator, and set the legs aside for curing. Trim off all excess fat from the carcasses, placing it in a saucepan. Set the carcasses aside to make stock. Melt the fat in the saucepan over low heat until completely liquefied. Pour fat into a bowl or jar and refrigerate until ready to use.

To cure the duck legs: Place them in a casserole or other dish that fits them well. Combine sugar, salt, and remaining cure ingredients in a bowl. Pour the cure into the casserole, coat the legs well with the mixture, and turn them skin side up. Cover the casserole loosely with plastic wrap and weight down the contents with a plate and some cans or a brick. Refrigerate for 2 to 3 days.

Meanwhile, make the duck stock. Preheat oven to 350°F. Roast the duck carcasses in a shallow roasting pan or dish for 1 hour, or until well browned. Remove from the oven. While the roasting pan cools, place the roasted carcasses in a large (approximately 15-quart) stockpot. Cover with water and bring to a boil. Skim off any impurities that come to the top. Reduce heat to a simmer and cook slowly for 1 hour. Roughly chop onion, celery, and carrot. Add vegetables, garlic, bay leaves and peppercorns to the stock and simmer for ½ hour more. Strain stock and refrigerate.

For the confit, about 4 cups of duck fat will be needed. If the amount on hand seems short, duck fat is available at fine grocers or online. Duck fat may be reused many times.

When ready to *confire* (make the conserve), preheat the oven to 275°F. Remove duck legs from the casserole, rinse under cold water to remove remaining cure, and pat dry. Place them in a roasting pan and cover with melted duck fat. Cover with foil and cook for 3 hours or until meat is falling off the bone. Allow to cool to room temperature. (Confit in this way, the duck in its fat will keep for a long time and may be reheated for serving as is.) For use in the ragù, pull the meat from the bones, shred, and reserve.

To make the duck ragù: Rehydrate porcini mushrooms in warm water for 20 minutes. Pour a splash of vegetable oil into a Dutch oven or large saucepan, set over medium-low heat. Cut onion into 1/2-inch dice, add to the Dutch oven, and sweat. Chop rehydrated mushrooms and add to the onion, cooking for a few minutes before adding the garlic. Cook for a few more minutes, then add tomatoes and simmer gently for 7–8 minutes. Deglaze pan with red wine and reduce until almost dry. Add 4 cups of the duck stock and simmer until reduced by half, or until it has the consistency of heavy cream. Stir in shredded duck confit. Season with salt and pepper to taste, and reserve.

To prepare the duck breasts: Place breasts skin side up on a cutting board. Using a sharp boning knife, score the duck skin in a crosshatch pattern. Be careful not to cut into the meat. Season with salt and pepper and flip over so the flesh side is up. Carefully trim any silver skin away.

Place a sauté pan over low heat and add duck breasts, skin side down. Render the fat until duck skin is well browned and crispy and no gooey fat remains. Turn over and roast for 4–5 minutes until internal temperature is 145°F (for medium rare).

Remove from pan and allow to rest on a plate for 10 minutes. Reserve rendered fat for future use.

To make the polenta: Bring 3 quarts of water to a simmer over medium heat in a large (15-quart) stockpot. Slowly whisk in 1 pound of instant polenta and cook slowly until thick(ish). Stir in cheese and butter, and season aggressively with salt and black pepper.

To serve: Choose shallow bowls. Into each, spoon polenta, and top with a ladle of ragù. Slice duck breast across the grain and arrange on top of the ragù.

VIGNOLA

10 DANA STREET
(207) 772-1330
WWW.VIGNOLAMAINE.COM
CHEF: LEE SKAWINSKI
OWNER: DAN KARY

Tucked behind pillars of leafy vines, just a few cobbled steps from the waterfront in the Old Port, Vignola is a classic Italian *osteria,* serving wines from an impeccable list of international offerings and light meals of cheeses, charcuterie, hearth-oven-baked pizzas, and assorted antipasti. Around the corner from their acclaimed Cinque Terre restaurant (page 48), Chef Lee Skawinski and partner Dan Kary bring to Vignola the same meticulous attention to detail: cured meats range from truffled pork liver to duck

rillettes, antipasti include beef carpaccio with greens and fried capers and Winter Point oysters with prosecco mignonette, and the cheese list is comprised of dozens of offerings, from creamy robiola to pungent blue. Their popular Sunday brunch has been called "Italian comfort" by *Down East* magazine, and it brings together Italian ingredients in an American form—think ricotta pancakes topped with Maine maple syrup, or deviled eggs with smoked scallops and cornichons.

As at Cinque Terre, many of the ingredients in Vignola's kitchen are grown on the restaurant's own Grand View Farm, and every autumn, patrons are invited to meet at Vignola for a day at the farm, which culminates in the annual Harvest Dinner. In an intimate afternoon, visitors explore the farm while enjoying appetizers and aperitifs al fresco, before enjoying a meal crafted from the season's freshest ingredients.

WINTER SQUASH SFORMATINO WITH BRA CHEESE FONDUTA

(SERVES 4)

For the sformatino:

1 cup roasted and pureed heirloom squash
4 large eggs
2 ounces heavy cream
1 cup ricotta cheese
½ teaspoon nutmeg
Salt and freshly ground black pepper to taste

4 8-ounce ramekins
Butter for greasing
4 teaspoons fine bread crumbs

For the sauce:

½ tablespoon butter
2 slices garlic
1 sprig thyme
1 leek, slit, well washed, and shredded
20 ounces heavy cream
1 cup grated Bra cheese
Salt and freshly ground black pepper, to taste

Preheat oven to 350°F. Mix squash, eggs, cream, ricotta, nutmeg, salt, and pepper in a bowl, and whisk until smooth. Butter four ramekins, put a teaspoon of bread crumbs in each, shake to coat the bottom and sides, and tap out any excess. Divide the squash mixture between the ramekins.

Place the ramekins in a sheet pan, pour 1 cup hot water around them, slide the pan into the oven, and bake for 15–20 minutes or until set.

In a small saucepan over medium heat, place the butter, garlic, and thyme, and cook for 30 seconds. Add the leeks and sweat for 2 minutes, then add the cream and simmer for 15 minutes.

The leeks should look melted. Stir the cheese in, a third at a time, and when it is incorporated, season to taste with salt and pepper.

On each of four small appetizer plates, place a tablespoon of sauce. Invert a ramekin over the plate and allow the *sformatino* to release. Pour a bit more sauce on top and serve.

DEERING OAKS

Designed by architect William A. Goodwin in conjunction with Frederick Law Olmsted, Deering Oaks Park is one of Portland's most scenic spots, perfect for a picnic or a stroll. Listed on the National Register of Historic Places, the fifty-five-acre park was built in 1879 on the site of a famed 1689 battle between British, French, and Native Americans, and now combines areas of natural beauty with public tennis and basketball courts, a playground, an outdoor stage, a large pond, a historic castle (currently maintained as a visitor's center by the Convention and Visitors Bureau), and manicured gardens. The park's beloved Rose Circle is one of the few public gardens in the United States allowed by the American Rose Society to preview its All-American Rose varieties, planting roses each year that aren't yet on the market for public sale. Lively all year round, the park is home in summer to theater productions and a weekly farmers' market, while winter sees pickup games of hockey and trees lit with twinkling lights.

Vinland

WWW.VINLAND.ME
CHEF/OWNER: DAVID LEVI

A native of New York City, Chef David Levi fell in love with the flavors of Maine on trips up from the city to visit the family of an old girlfriend. Years later, after refining his culinary skills in the kitchens of Jean-Georges Vongerichten's Perry Street, Fäviken Magasinet in northern Sweden, and Copenhagen's famed Noma, and studying with acclaimed Tuscan butchers Stefano Falorni and Dario Cecchini, Chef Levi returned to Maine full time.

Vinland, the Viking term for a region that included what's now the state of Maine, combines Chef Levi's many interests and influences, from Scandinavian cuisine to the raw foods advocated by Weston A. Price. Currently a "pop up" restaurant, Vinland's permanent location is one of the most anticipated arrivals on the Portland food scene. Using ingredients sourced exclusively in the state, Chef Levi's menus celebrate cured and aged meats, fermented vegetables, dried and salted produce and meats, and raw food. Despite a love of olive oil instilled by his Italian father, Chef Levi uses exclusively oils that are produced in Maine, such as butters and rendered animal fats, and in lieu of kitchen staples like citrus and black pepper, he experiments with vinegars, ferments, and pungent local herbs. As at Noma, much of what's found on the ever-changing menu is foraged, and Chef Levi can be spotted scouring the sides of Bradbury Mountain in search of black trumpet mushrooms, reindeer lichen, juniper berries, and the branches that will make up much of the restaurant's décor. Incorporating the Scandinavian aesthetic, Vinland is both earthy and spare, serving many of its dishes perched atop rocks and on beds of moss.

The Liver Tartare and Cranberry on Celery Chips is a local twist on the steak tartare Chef Levi learned to prepare in Tuscany. Don't be put off by the idea of eating raw beef liver; its creamy texture is surprisingly light, and the vivid colors make a beautifully bright contrast with the celery chip. You will have more cranberry sauce than you need for this recipe, but it keeps beautifully in the refrigerator for up to two weeks and can be used as a condiment with poultry, meats, and hearty vegetables (try it with Pepperclub's Harvest Vegetable Loaf, page 137). For a delicious variation on the leftover sauce, add fresh grated ginger root, to taste.

The crisp reindeer lichen in Vinland's Shrimp on Lichen with Kale and Maitake has the texture of toast. When sourcing it, be sure to work with a knowledgeable, trusted forager. Maine shrimp are tiny, with a sweet, delicate flavor that nicely balances the earthiness of the dish's other ingredients. If Maine shrimp aren't available, substitute another wild-caught American shrimp instead of the large jumbo, which will overpower the other flavors and textures. For best results, Chef Levi strongly suggests that all ingredients be organic and, whenever possible, locally sourced.

LIVER TARTARE & CRANBERRY ON CELERY CHIPS

(SERVES 6)

6 ounces raw cleaned beef liver (see note)
2 tablespoons fresh herbs—rosemary, plus oregano,
    marjoram, and/or sage
1 small clove garlic
½ teaspoon sea salt, or more, to taste
2 ounces ghee (clarified butter)

1 cup fresh cranberries
¼ cup apple cider, preferably unpasteurized
2 tablespoons maple syrup, or more, to taste
2 teaspoons apple cider vinegar
⅛ teaspoon sea salt

1 large celery root
½ pound ghee (clarified butter)
Sea salt for dusting

1 cup dried black trumpet mushroom
2 tablespoons sea salt

To prepare the tartare, mince raw beef liver finely,
taking care to remove connective tissue and fat.
Mince or puree herbs and garlic with salt. In a
bowl, mix liver with herbs. Set aside.

In a small saucepan, melt 2 ounces ghee over
very low heat. Making sure the pan is warm—not
hot—fold liver mixture into the ghee. Liver must
not cook, but ghee should remain in a liquid state
to properly blend.

In the bowl of a food processor, combine
cranberries, apple cider, maple syrup, apple cider
vinegar, and sea salt and puree until smooth.

Using a mandoline or a meat slicer, slice celery
root into thin rounds. Dry the rounds in direct
sunlight, a dehydrator, or an oven set to 200°F.
When celery root rounds have dried, melt
½ pound ghee in a small saucepan and bring it
to 300°F. Working in small batches, flash fry the
dried celery root rounds for not more than 10
seconds. Place on paper towels to drain, and
dust lightly with sea salt, if desired.

Using a well-cleaned spin coffee grinder,
pulverize the dried black trumpet mushrooms
and sea salt, adding mushrooms a little at a time
if they don't all fit.

To assemble: Spoon a dollop of liver onto a celery
chip, topping with about half as much cranberry
sauce. Dust with mushroom salt and serve on a
clean stone.

Note: For ease and maximum food safety
(though at some loss in texture), raw liver may be
sliced into discs and frozen on a baking sheet.
When completely frozen, pack liver into airtight
bags and leave frozen at −40°F for 14 days. If
using this method, some connective tissue
may be left, and liver may be minced while still
somewhat frozen.

Shrimp on Lichen with Kale & Maitake

(SERVES 6)

8 ounces kale

¼ cup unsalted butter

1 clove garlic

¾ pound ghee (clarified butter)

¼ pound Maine shrimp, cleaned

2 ounces fresh maitake (hen-of-the-woods) mushrooms

Reindeer lichen (see note)

Sea salt

Puree kale—leaves and stems—with butter. Spread mixture in a thin layer on parchment paper or silicon mats and dry either in direct sunlight or in a dehydrator at 155°F. If necessary, the mixture may be dried in an oven on the lowest possible setting, checking frequently to prevent burning. When kale is completely dry and brittle, break it up with your hands so it can be used as a topping.

Slice garlic into thick rounds. In a large sauté pan over low heat, melt 1 tablespoon ghee. Add garlic and cook, removing and discarding at first sign of browning. Add shrimp and cook until barely opaque. Place shrimp in a chilled bowl.

Break maitake into small, attractive fronds. In a medium sauté pan, heat 1–2 tablespoons ghee and cook mushrooms until lightly browned and somewhat crisp.

Clean lichen of forest debris and break into pieces roughly 1½ to 2 inches square and up to 1 inch thick. In a large saucepan, bring remaining ghee to 300°F. Bring a large pot of water to a boil and parboil the lichen for 10 seconds. Remove lichen from water, pat dry, and fry in the hot ghee for about 15 seconds until crisp but not browned.

To serve: Place shrimp on lichen, top with a dusting of kale and one small maitake frond. Serve on a clean stone.

Note: Reindeer lichen may be foraged in northern woods or ordered online, though more likely from hobby suppliers than from food purveyors. For maximum safety, specify when buying that the lichen will be used for culinary purposes.

Zapoteca Restaurante y Tequileria

505 Fore Street
(207) 772-8242
WWW.ZAPOTECARESTAURANT.COM
Chef/Owner: Shannon Bard
Co-Owners: Tom Bard and Sergio Ramos

Growing up in Oklahoma, Chef Shannon Bard spent long hours with her family around the table enjoying meals prepared by her grandmother, who owned a Mexican restaurant. Joining her grandmother in the kitchen, Chef Bard learned to make these meals at her side, incorporating produce grown on the small farms of her father and grandfather, who instilled in her a respect for the hard work and dedication they put into every crop. Years later, after graduating from the Culinary Institute of America in San Antonio, Texas, Chef Bard, her husband Tom, and longtime friend and tequila expert Sergio Ramos brought their passion for authentic Mexican cooking north, opening Zapoteca Restaurante y Tequileria.

Named for the Zapotecs, an indigenous people of Mexico, the restaurant celebrates their tradition of slow cooking over hot coals, creating meals and sauces like the famed mole using techniques that date back centuries. Chef Bard starts every dish from

simple ingredients, incorporating Maine's local products whenever possible, and bringing out flavors with techniques such as dry-roasting. Sergio Ramos brings his expertise with spirits—specifically tequila—to the bar, mixing inventive cocktails and guiding patrons through flights of imported tequilas, broken up by a zesty tomato palate cleanser.

As a team, the trio balance one another, a fact they playfully note with their logo of three Mexican masks. According to the owners, each mask represents an element of their characters: Chef Bard, like her dancing mask, is always on the go, moving her feet around the kitchen; Tom Bard, like the bull, is knowledgeable and strong willed; and Sergio Ramos, like the strong man, brings a steady desire for authenticity. Together they create bold flavors in a warm atmosphere, bringing a little kick to the Old Port.

For the Tortas de Jaiba con Salsa Poblano, Chef Bard dry-roasts several ingredients. A standard technique in the Oaxacan kitchen, she notes: "Dry-roasting

is an amazingly simple technique that is essential to recreating the flavors of Mexican cuisine. When dry-roasted, vegetables and chilies will have an intense flavor and even a slight bitterness imparted by the char. To dry-roast: heat a cast iron pan or other flat, heavy skillet over medium-high heat. Do not be tempted to add oil to the skillet, as the pan must be dry and free from all oil. For the recipe below, add the onion (peeled and quartered) and unpeeled garlic clove to the skillet, turning frequently until browned but still slightly crisp. Transfer to a cutting board and, once cool enough to handle, coarsely chop the onion and peel the garlic."

When making the Watermelon Habanero Margarita, you'll need a 10-ounce cocktail shaker with a strainer, and a muddler or large spoon. Watermelon concentrate is available at most groceries, but if you can't find it, simply puree a few seeded watermelon cubes in the food processor.

Tortas de Jaiba con Salsa Poblano

Serrano Crab Cakes with Poblano Cream Sauce

(SERVES 6)

For the poblano cream sauce:

3 medium poblano chilies
6 tablespoons dry-roasted onion
1 dry-roasted clove garlic
¾ cup crema fresca or crème fraiche
¾ cup half-and-half
1 teaspoon oregano, preferably Mexican
½ teaspoon salt
⅛ teaspoon cinnamon

For the crab cakes:

4 small tomatillos, husked, rinsed, and
    finely chopped (approximately ½ cup)
⅓ cup chopped fresh cilantro
3 tablespoons thinly sliced scallions, white and
    green parts
1 tablespoon finely chopped celery
5 tablespoons seeded and minced serrano chilies
¼ teaspoon salt
1 pound fresh crabmeat
2 large eggs, beaten
2 tablespoons poblano cream sauce
2 cups panko bread crumbs
½ cup olive oil

For the poblano "angel hair":

2 poblano chili peppers, dry-roasted and skinned
2 cups all-purpose flour
2 teaspoons salt
⅛ teaspoon black pepper
¼ teaspoon cayenne pepper
½ cup canola oil

6 cilantro leaves, for garnish
3 radishes, julienned, for garnish

To make the poblano cream sauce: Place all ingredients in a blender and puree until extremely smooth. Chill until ready to use.

To make the serrano crab cakes: Mix together tomatillos, cilantro, scallions, celery, chilies, and salt in a large bowl. Stir in crabmeat. Add the eggs, 2 tablespoons poblano cream sauce, and 1 cup bread crumbs. Shape crabmeat mixture into 6 cakes, each about 1 inch thick. Gently coat the crab cakes on both sides with the remaining 1 cup of bread crumbs.

Preheat oven to 375°F, and position a rack in the top third of the oven. In a large nonstick skillet or sauté pan over medium-high heat, heat the olive oil until it shimmers. Working in batches, add the crab cakes to the pan and cook until lightly browned on the bottom, about 1 minute. Turn and brown the other side of each cake. Using a slotted spatula, transfer to paper towels to drain, then place on a baking sheet. Bake the crab cakes in the preheated oven until heated through, 7–10 minutes.

To make the poblano "angel hair": Slice the roasted and skinned poblanos very thinly with a very sharp knife. Place in a baking dish and cover tightly.

In a bowl, combine flour, salt, pepper, and cayenne. Set aside.

When ready to cook, heat canola oil to 350°F in a deep skillet. Take ½ cup of prepared poblano chilies, cover well with the flour mixture, shake off the excess, and plunge into hot oil. Fry until golden and drain on a rack lined with paper towels.

To assemble the dish: Spoon approximately 2 ounces of sauce into the bottom of each serving bowl. Top with a crab cake. Pile poblano "angel hair" on top of the crab cake and garnish with cilantro leaf and julienned radish.

Perfect Pairing

WATERMELON HABANERO MARGARITA

(MAKES 1 COCKTAIL)

½ fresh lime

Coarse sugar

7 (1-inch) cubes watermelon

⅛-inch slice fresh habanero chili pepper

1 ounce freshly squeezed lime juice

1 ounce Citronage or good-quality orange liqueur

2½ ounces good-quality white tequila

½ ounce watermelon concentrate or finely pureed watermelon

Ice cubes

Moisten the rim of a 6-ounce martini glass with the cut side of the lime half. Spread coarse sugar on a small plate and upend the glass into the sugar to crust the rim.

Place 4 cubes of watermelon in the shaker along with the slice of habanero pepper. Using a cocktail muddler or the back side of a large spoon, grind together the watermelon and habanero slice to form a rough paste. Half fill the shaker with ice. Measure in the lime juice, orange liqueur, tequila, and watermelon concentrate. Shake for about 15 seconds. Strain and pour into prepared martini glass. Garnish with additional 3 watermelon cubes.

Recipe Index

General Index

About the Author & Photographer

Margaret Hathaway is the author of The *Year of the Goat, Living with Goats,* and *Food Lovers' Guide to Maine.* Photographer **Karl Schatz** is the Director of Aurora Photos and the leader of Slow Food Portland Maine. The couple lives with their three children on a small farm in southern Maine, where they raise dairy goats and poultry, tend a large garden and small orchard, make cheese, and teach homesteading workshops. Visit them at TenAppleFarm.com.

Photo by Greta Rybus